"Why does this book speak to so many people? Jim and I pondered this as we read through the pages that put us in the middle of Andy's journey and compelled us again to reexamine what God is asking of our lives. Andy's journey will simply speak to you because his experience translates to everyone's need to understand the unfathomable designs of God. The answer may be that we can never fully understand God's complete plan, but in our desire to comprehend God's will for us in the moment, day by day, we can find healing and peace just as Andy experienced. As Jim and I looked back on our own journey with God and faith, we started thinking back to the first time we met Andy at the Boston Men's Conference in 2010. Again, you ask yourself, what draws anyone to speak with this person over another. Possibly it isn't coincidence at all, but God's design, part of that unfathomable plan. We are all meant to be part of other people's journey to help them get where they need to go. Our small part in Andy's journey was Jim trying to get Andy to go to Medjugorje for the first time. My husband, Jim, recognized in Andy a kindred spirit of tremendous drive, a relentless persistence. Jim knew how important Medjugorje had been to his spiritual growth, and he used this relentless persistence to prod Andy into going. Jim saw in Andy that same restless longing for God that he had felt. It is that restless longing that allows us the opportunity to find union with Christ if we choose to take it. Andy not only chose to take that chance, but he has used his experience to help others through his writing. Andy's soul searching book touched us both because of its central theme of transforming love; a transforming love that we wish for all who take the time to read this thought provoking story."
Jim and Kerri Caviezel

"The past decade of Andy LaVallee's life shows the power of Men's Conferences, the impact of good Catholic friendships, the help of the Blessed Mother to draw near to Christ Jesus, the power of fasting, and the positive impact of Catholic social teaching in the workplace. We are fortunate in the Archdiocese of Boston to have leaders such as Andy LaVallee who actively reach out to invite others to experience the joy of living as a disciple within the Catholic community."
Cardinal Sean O'Malley, Archdiocese of Boston

"If you want to make God laugh; make plans." Anyone journeying through a life of faith will agree with that old saying including my friend Andy LaVallee. His story is a powerful example of what Romans 8:28 looks like in real life. Who knew that a bustling baking business would eventually be a recipe that feeds not only bodies but souls? God did and I'm just glad, despite the many questions and challenges along the way, that Andy said 'yes.'"
Teresa Tomeo, Motivational Speaker, Best-Selling Author,
Syndicated Catholic Talk Show Host
www.teresatomeo.com

"Every man, particularly Catholic man, should read this story of how Andy was led from fast living to living the fast. His story has resonance for everyone who grew up in a tough neighborhood, then achieved worldly success and wondered if that level of impact and happiness was all there was in life. Was it their true purpose? Andy's honest, humble and entertaining storytelling will ensure that all readers will like and learn from this great book."
Scot Landry, Boston Catholic Men's Conference
GoodCatholicLeadership.com

In 1994, Saint John Paul II wrote: *"The whole of the Christian life is like a great pilgrimage to the house of the Father, whose unconditional love for every human creature [...] we discover anew each day."* That is the pilgrimage that Andrew LaVallee took and journeyed through. In this pilgrimage we each can experience the fullness of our conversion when the new life of faith from within intersects with the old world from without. For Andrew LaVallee, writing and publishing this journey is yet a testimony of his desire to reach the fullness of his conversion not only for himself but to share its grace with others. May God's Name be glorified and many people be inspired by this conversion pilgrimage and journey deeper into their own conversion through this book.
Mother Olga of the Sacred Heart,
Mother Servant and Foundress of Daughters of Mary of Nazareth

"From the Hub to the Heart" will give you a window into the life of a truly extraordinary man, a man who daily inspires me to live out the life that God intends for me, to be the best version of myself. As you turn the pages, I pray that you too will be inspired by Andy's message of hope. I pray that you too may give the Lord your "yes" as Andy did and continues to do daily."
Tim Van Damm, CHPT Construction Partner

"If you are a practical person, this book is the real deal. Andy's inspiration to start *Live the Fast* is nothing more than a reactivation of the early Christian regimen, as found in 'The Teaching of the Twelve Apostles,' the first Catholic Catechism, if you will, known as 'The Didache.' Don't wait. Just do it."
(Rev.) Thomas M. Hart, O.S.B.
Assistant to the President for Mission
Saint Vincent College, Latrobe, PA

"I am deeply moved by this story of profound conversion. And his message about fasting could not be more important – both for people who have not yet begun to fast and for those, like me, who so often try, but fail to fast well. Andy does not just speak about fasting, but through his wonderful ministry is actually doing something practical to help us all do this. I would encourage everyone to read this great book."
Magnus MacFarlane-Bar, Mary's Meals – Saving Grace

"God has chosen Andy LaVallee for a critical task of our time. The West has forgotten the power of fasting, which does nothing less than transform hearts, lives, and the course of nations. This fascinating book chronicles the true story of how Andy was plucked from his rough and tumble beginnings in the bank-robbing capital of America, saved from his over-indulgent worldly appetites, dusted off and cleaned up by Our Lord and the Blessed Mother in Medjugorje, and fashioned into a holy and loveable apostle of fasting. Pick up this book, take it to heart, and enjoy the ride of *your* life."
Christine Watkins, MTS, LCSW, Catholic speaker, media host, and author of *Full of Grace: Miraculous Stories of Healing and Conversion through Mary's Intercession*

"Andy LaVallee is a remarkable man. And his story is a powerful one, sure to inspire and move everyone who reads it!"
Allen Hunt, Best-Selling Author and Speaker, Dynamic Catholic Institute

"I'm really grateful to Andy LaVallee for his book. *I need it! I'm reading it. I love it!* Our Lady tells us in her messages, 'God *doesn't want anything from you, only your surrender.*' Andy's surrender is helping me. "
Denis Nolan, Mary TV   www.marytv.tv

"Andy's open-hearted 'call it like I see it' courage is a refreshing virtue. It's exceptionally easy to read a story about a person who is this honest with himself."
Charlie Fox, owner of Friendbox

"Andy LaVallee'e book is so important. Inspired by Medjugorje and Fr. Slavko specifically, Andy shows us the way. He offers practical guidance and leads us towards higher goals and encounters with the Lord."
Fr. Jozo Grbeš, Pastor Saint Jerome Parish Archdiocese of Chicago, Head of the Croatian Franciscans of US and Canada

From the Hub to the Heart
My Journey

By

Andrew LaVallee
with Leticia Velasquez

Spiritual Advisor: Father Sean Morris OMV

Cover Design by Venanzio at Tatlin.net
Editing/Formatting: Ellen Gable Hrkach

Published on February 11, 2015, Feast of Our Lady of Lourdes

To purchase copies of this book:
livethefast.org

Live the Fast
117 Beaver Street
Waltham, MA 02452

livethefast.org

Purpose
"To point more people to eternity through my personal conversion and stories."

Dedication

To the Queen of Peace

and

To my loving family:
Barbara,
Jeff and Mian, Nicole and Joe
and my grandchildren

Table of Contents

Foreword
Jack O'Callahan

Jack O'Callahan is a member of the 1980 USA Hockey Team
that defeated the Soviet Union in the Famous 'Miracle on Ice.'

I was quite touched when Andy asked me to pen the forward of his book. My first thought was, "So Andy is writing a book, hmmmmm, that's interesting because I'm not sure if he's ever read one!" Then I thought, "Maybe it's a coloring book so it could be fun."

Before you think that this guy O'Callahan is the biggest jerk God ever created, understand that the opening paragraph of my introduction is just a little private joke and — trust me — Andy is laughing.

Andy LaVallee and I grew up in an environment where gentle teasing was pretty common, and we all learned at a young age that a sense of humor is an invaluable attribute. Now well into our fifth and even sixth decade of life, it's our ability to laugh at ourselves and at life's curve balls that keeps the stress manageable and gives us the strength to soldier on.

Andy and I grew up together in Charlestown, Massachusetts, a little one-square-mile historic district on the north side of Boston where they fought the Battle of Bunker Hill, and where the seeds of our great nation were initially planted back in the late 1700's. As children of Charlestown, we learned to love our country.

We came of age in the 1960's and 70's, got married, and began raising our families in the 1980's and 90's and here we are in the new millennium. Andy and his wife, the amazing Barbara, are grandparents and the world keeps turning.

Andy and I were raised by parents who grew up together in that same town, but in the 1930's, 40's and 50's. Like us, they played sports together, went to church together, fought with each other, loved each other, saw each other have successes and failures, and witnessed all forms of highs and lows. They were raised in the Depression years prior to World War II and into the Korean War. They were teenagers when bombs dropped on Hiroshima and Nagasaki and, after that, lived for a long time through the Cold War wondering when or where the next one would fall; would it be New York City or Moscow? They lived with fear, but they had no fear and embraced life. They loved their families, loved their community, they soldiered on, loved their Lord and got through each day with an unshakeable faith that was both inspiring and awesome. They passed it forward and we, as their children, were and are blessed.

Our parents' generation saw their friend's children head off to Vietnam and saw other friend's children head off to protest that same war. They as parents and us as children saw the beginnings of the drug and anti-establishment culture, the technology boom, and the many changes to society driven by the Baby Boom generation of which Andy and I are a part.

Charlestown had a respected and even feared reputation for all those years, not only around Boston, but also around

Massachusetts, around New England, and even around the nation. There was a rough element but also strong athletics and great athletes. It was a place of deep pride, incredible politics, great neighborhoods, blue collar tradesmen, firemen, policemen, and tight-knit families. There were hardscrabble union members and tough and uncompromising labor leaders. It was a place of unbreakable connections where solid friendships like that which Andy, I, and our families have shared for close to seventy-five years could grow upon solid foundations. Even the bad kids had souls and even the bad kids were good kids inside. We are Townies at heart and Townies never give up and never lose hope. At its essence, that's who we are.

Most of all, the Charlestown of my and Andy's youth and the youthful years of our parents was a place of faith and community. There were always three Catholic parishes: Saint Francis, Saint Catherine's, and Saint Mary's. One square mile, three parishes. Our predominately Irish-Catholic homeland was defined by the teachings of the Catholic Church. The priests and nuns were held in high esteem, respected and supported. Along with our parents, they raised us and nurtured us.

It was in this place where the roots of Andy's strong faith took hold. When Andy's dad had a heart attack and tragically passed away at a young age, Andy was compelled to become a man all too soon. It was difficult for his mom, for him, for his brother Bobby, my close childhood friend who was at a very impressionable age, and his younger brother Arty who was barely into his teens. Those were hard times for the LaVallees and there was no magic wand. As a family, they had to find a way and they did. God love them for it.

In all the ensuing years, the three things that guided Andy were his hopefulness, his work ethic and his faith. He had successes and made mistakes like we all do and he and his brothers had their ups and downs, but they soldiered on knowing that God is good and Andy always had hope.

13

After college, life took me away from Boston and Charlestown as my professional hockey and business career nudged me towards Chicago. When Andy and I reconnected as adults and reaffirmed our friendship many years later, it was Andy's faith that was still there. It was incredible to reconnect; I was lifted up. Even though we hadn't seen each other in fifteen years, it was as if we had seen each other the day before. What struck me immediately was the strength of his character, and it was right out front like a tattoo on his forehead. I was truly inspired and felt reconnected to my childhood, my parents, my friends, my community, and my faith.

Through all those years, Andy kept smiling, kept laughing, occasionally crying, but never losing hope, never doubting. He was a rock; a true rock and he remains so today.

As you read this book, this collection of stories and life experiences documented by an amazing man, please keep this thought in your heart. Andy LaVallee is a man of principle, a man of strength, a man of character, a man of hope, and a man with great heart. He has been teaching C.C.D. to young, at-risk teens since he himself was a young man. Whenever life got challenging for him and Barbara, he never turned his back on others in need. He has been reaching out through his incredible bread business to support families, and he has changed lives for the better across generations by sharing his spirit, his passion, and his tremendous thoughtfulness and caring.

I have been blessed with many things in my life and I am very thankful. My friendship with Andy is a blessing that stands out and energizes me with an appreciation of the wonder of life, the wonder of community, the wonder of family, and the wonder of faith. Andy continues to extend his hand to make God's kingdom on earth a better place for all whom he encounters. I love him for it because I know that his friendship and his presence in my life have made me a better person, a better parent, a better husband, and a better friend.

My wish for you as a reader is that you are able to open your heart to experience Andy's incredible spirit as I have. He is truly one of a kind. He is a big hunk of heart and soul and, on a daily basis, I am thankful to have him in my life.

Good friends rock the world like nothing else and Andy rocks my world.

I love you, Bud, you're the bomb. Never stop being you.

Enjoy the ride, everyone.

"Littera Scripta Manet"
The Written Word Endures
Jack O'Callahan

Introduction

Leticia Velasquez

"Do not be afraid to cast yourselves into the arms of God; whatever He asks of you, he will repay a hundredfold. "

Pope Francis

So many people long to have a relationship with God. They feel a need to experience the love and peace which the world cannot give them, but they fear one thing: that God will make demands of them to change their lifestyle, give up certain habits, give more time to prayer, end unhealthy, sinful relationships, spend money differently and, most of all, take their emphasis off "what gives me pleasure" and replace it with "what pleases God." They are not convinced that what God has in store for them will be as good as what they think is good now. They fear being bored and stifled by the Church. So they sigh a deep sigh of regret like the rich young man whom Christ asked to give up his worldly goods, follow Him, and walk away. They have no idea what they are giving up.

Andy LaVallee was that rich young man. He had a multi-million dollar international bread distribution business. He was an amazing amateur golfer, high rolling gambler and racehorse owner, with a hard-earned reputation for excellence in everything he did. He drove fine cars; he drank hard, played hard, travelled the world and enjoyed the company of some of the world's most powerful people. He had earned it all with unceasing dedication to his goals from the age of twenty when the sudden death of his father after an argument left Andy with a burning desire to prove to the world that he could make something of himself. He wanted to prove that he could leave the corrupt world of

Charlestown, one of Boston's neighborhoods, bank robbing capital of America, and become a world class businessman. In a little over two decades, he achieved a truly amazing level of success. He was living the dream, yet somehow there was still emptiness in his heart. A God-shaped hole in his heart. As Saint Augustine, another rich young man who had the world at his feet but knew no peace said, "Our hearts are restless until they rest in Thee."

This book tells the story of what happened when a movie star known for his portrayal of Jesus Christ in *The Passion of the Christ*, Jim Caviezel, looked into this successful man's eyes one day and challenged him just as Christ challenged the rich young man. He dared Andy to visit Medjugorje, an obscure, poor village in Croatia, where for over thirty years it has been alleged that the Virgin Mary has been visiting earth and calling her children to live lives of prayer, penance and fasting. Andy's first reaction was predictable; "No way am I flying fifteen hours to pray a Rosary!" But little by little, Our Lady's call to Andy opened his heart and he boarded that plane, prayed that Rosary and his life has never been the same.

Chapter 1
Growing Up In Charlestown

My relationship with my dad was always a rocky one, fueled by me constantly seeking his approval. In our house sometimes it felt like a losing battle. We were constantly fighting, and there were many verbal threats by both of us. I think in some ways, as much as I was disappointed in him, Dad was very disappointed in me. He was my father and I loved him, but I really never felt like a priority in his life, even though I was his oldest son of three boys. There were many times he had been drinking with his friends in a local tavern, and my brothers and I were left in the car all alone for hours wondering when he would come out. I wanted so badly to be one of those friends! During my high school years, I played traditional varsity sports like baseball, basketball and some pick-up hockey. He never attended a game, even if it was a playoff or an important game. Growing up in this violent neighborhood of Charlestown, I desperately needed him in my life. When I could not convince him to attend a high school basketball or baseball game, I started to look elsewhere for approval. I had to deal with the pain somehow, but how?

It was a hot and hazy summer morning in Boston, August 2, 1975. I was twenty years old, newly married and working for Quinzani Bakery delivering bread on third shift. After finishing work that morning, I visited my parents for breakfast. The evening before, I was over at my brother's place drinking and playing cards, and somehow my father got wind of it. After leaving my brother's house without any sleep, I had worked the third shift, and I was driving my work truck to my parents' house for breakfast at 8:30. That day was my father's first day of a five-week vacation. I had never known him to take a vacation or even a day off. He definitely deserved it. He was the sole provider for me, my mom and my two brothers, and I sometimes wondered, "How does he do it?"

My dad was a veteran of the Korean War and a much-disciplined individual. He would always tell me, especially when I was defiant, "Wait until they get you in the Army!" As luck would turn out, the week after I got my draft card, the U.S. government abolished the draft. I think he was right, though, that I would have benefited from that type of discipline.

That day was a scorcher, over 100 degrees and, that afternoon, Dad was going on a fishing trip with his buddies. I was visiting my parents in the home I grew up in, the triple-decker brick brownstone 300 yards from Saint Francis de Sales Church on 294 Bunker Hill Street in Charlestown. I parked the truck, walked up two flights of stairs and saw my mom cooking in the kitchen and my dad sitting down drinking coffee. I walked in and said, "Hi, Dad." Right off the bat, he started with me. "I'm not going to be around to bail you out all the time. By the way, you are never going to amount to anything unless you get squared away." I had just turned twenty and had gotten married; my wife and I had paid for our own wedding by working two jobs. Dad was worried about my life in general, and he certainly was not impressed when he heard I played cards and stayed up all night delivering bread.

Most kids in my neighborhood had been arrested by the time they were sixteen and were totally against any authority. I had been in serious trouble but never got fingerprinted. During recent years, my dad and I had a really

20

explosive relationship. My parents would have brutal battles stimulated by alcohol, with furniture being broken or police showing up because it got too loud. So, trying to avoid an argument, I said, "Whatever, Dad. I am sick of this," and went into the kitchen to give my mom a kiss. My dad was not going to drop the topic and soon our disagreement escalated. The last time this happened, he threw a cantaloupe fastball off the back of my head and knocked me over as I was going down the stairs. This time, I returned the barrage by yelling back. My mom was crying. Finally I screamed, "Dad, I can never satisfy you!" I walked out on breakfast and left.

Every time this happened, I was crushed by both our actions. I felt like these events totally separated us. I yelled many times in frustration with this relationship by telling him, "Just go be with your buddies." I went home to my apartment, took a nap and went to a barbeque with my wife's family. I never saw my father alive again.

At three in the afternoon, I got a phone call from my brother Bobby. "You got to get to Massachusetts General Hospital real quick! Dad had a heart attack!" At that point, I knew that my father had died; I felt it in my heart. This was his second heart attack; he had had one a few years before.

I got to the hospital and everybody was crying. I saw Mom, my brothers, my aunts, uncles and cousins, and I knew that he was gone. My uncle approached me and said, "Your father has passed away." So I went to seek out the doctor. I told him who I was. "I need to see my father." After he smelled the alcohol on me, he said, "No, you're not going to see your father." I replied, "You don't understand," and I told him what happened in the morning. I begged him, "I need to see my father, please. " So the doctor said, "Okay, come with me." And he brought me to a room to see the dead body of my father. I removed the sheet to see his face. I knelt, I prayed for him, and to him, asking for forgiveness. I cried and cried and cried, and thought about the argument we had just had. It was surreal and I could not understand it. So that was the event which defined things for me. For decades I carried the burden of my father's death and how I had contributed to it.

The day after my father died, I looked around and saw evidence that his death might destroy our whole family, so I told myself, "I'm going to be the best son, the best older brother I can be. I am going to assist my mom." I assumed Dad's position as head of the family. Mom did not even have a driver's license; my dad did everything for her. My younger brothers rejected me in that role; my middle brother Bobby was seventeen and a city champion swimmer. He got a pretty good start being six feet six inches tall. My youngest brother Arty was fifteen, and you could have nicknamed him 'the mayor' because he had so many friends. They both enjoyed a very different experience than I had with my dad, maybe because I was the oldest.

My father was waked at Tom Kelleher's Funeral Parlor in Somerville; Tom was one of my father's friends. In those days, wakes were two to four p.m. and six to eight p.m., two days in a row. Between those two times, people would come back to the house for drinks and food before returning to the wake. I couldn't leave the funeral parlor both days. My dad was going to be buried in two days and I didn't want to let go. I met each person who came to that casket and I shook every single hand. I wanted them to know I was Arthur LaVallee's oldest son Andrew. There were lines outside for blocks to get in and pay last respects to my dad who was only forty-six. I remember my mom asking me to give the eulogy. I declined, so my godfather Uncle Dick delivered it. I really should have given it, but I was afraid and still in shock. After two grueling days of wakes, the funeral was at Saint Francis de Sales Church right across the street from my house.

So here I was, trying to show everybody I was in charge. No one in my family or friends held me responsible for causing his death. But in my mind, I carried it with me every day: guilt and regret for the father-son relationship we never had. I told myself, "My hero is gone, so what am I going to do?"

Arthur J. LaVallee was a huge man, a friend to everyone. His nickname was Big A. My dad was really a drill sergeant in bakery gray overalls. He drove a truck for Bond Bread, and after he died, I saw the paystubs for his vacation and he was making only $110 per week. He wanted so much for us to have more than he had, and he was willing to do whatever it took to do it.

Here is the story that best describes my dad. When he died, I found out that he had taken out a bank loan for $5000, a pretty big loan for someone making such a small weekly salary. I phoned the bank and they said not to worry, that it had life insurance attached so it would be paid in full. I just couldn't figure it out, so I asked the bank representative to look up the reason behind the loan. He came back after a few minutes and said it was for his son's wedding. Then I remembered my father was so happy that day that he opened the bar for the entire wedding to serve all our friends and relatives a drink. He also gave us a significant gift to get started, all on a loan.

I went back to work and for about a year or so, I wallowed in my sorrow. I was a mess. As I was working, I was doing very regrettable things, constantly covering up for myself, but all the time, I was trying to figure it all out. I was going to church occasionally; my wife Barbara and I had been married at Saint Patrick's in Watertown on January 25, 1975. I was so grateful that I had my wife — she was so supportive — because we had just gone through the loss of her father who had died in February of 1974 of a cerebral hemorrhage, and he was only in his fifties. We had both lost our dads within a year; the two tragedies brought us much closer.

The city of Boston is divided up into neighborhoods. One of them is Charlestown, 15,000 people in one square mile. It is made up of mostly Irish Catholic blue collar workers: electricians, policemen, firemen, and longshoremen. Charlestown has another reputation: it's home to professional criminals and bank robbers, and it's known as the bank robbery capital of the world, as portrayed by the Ben Affleck film, "The Town." Guys from Charlestown, because of their success in crime, think they can get away with anything they want. Some of the attitudes you find in Charlestown go like this, "You can't stop me; I can get away with anything," and "You can't leave the 'Town.' You're stuck here with us."

I was born and raised in Charlestown, and until my conversion, it really defined me. Several of my friends tried to get out of 'Town.' Most their attempts resulted in a full scholarship to different state prisons. They were serious about not getting out.

There's a scene in the movie "The Town" where these guys are being brought in for questioning because they robbed a bank. The cops know they did the bank job, but they don't have any evidence, and the perps are basically flipping the cops off, playing them like a yo-yo. The cops are asking them questions and these guys are just toying with them, and they get away with it — only because they have the attitude that they think they can. And that was how it was; you think you can get away with everything.

When my friend, Jack O'Callahan, got a scholarship to Boston University to play hockey, he returned home to visit his parents for Thanksgiving, and some punk split his face wide open with a beer bottle to get him to react and escalate the fight into something more serious, like a knife or gun battle. Their efforts to keep Jack in the streets, like them, had failed. What they learned quickly was that Jack was smarter than that, and he had plans for his future, which did not include tangling with these punks.

I can remember one day a friend said to me, "Hey, we got the key to the Boston Garden Visitors' Locker Room." My friends and I never paid to see one event at the Garden: NHL Hockey, NBA basketball; we had various ways and connections to sneak into every game. The Bruins were going to play the Saint Louis Blues that night in hockey, but the game was delayed two hours because when the team arrived for the game to dress, the whole locker room was stripped clean. Jerseys, sticks, everything was gone! But these project kids were generous, they left the skates and, yes, it all ended up in the streets of Charlestown.

In our neighborhood it was always good against evil, and it seemed like evil was winning by a knockout. I can remember years ago playing golf with Jack O'Callahan and some friends. Jack was telling the story of how they beat the Russian Hockey Team in the famous 'Miracle Game' of the 1980 Olympics in Lake Placid. He said, "We had just all won the biggest victory in USA hockey history, and a few of the Charlestown wiseguys had found their way to Lake Placid and were trying to convince me to go out drinking and partying with them to celebrate." After that historic game, O.C. (which is Jack's lifelong nickname) was on a high, and he didn't need these guys to mess up his plans for a gold medal.

I had to be mentally tough growing up in Charlestown, because we lived in a war zone. Receiving black eyes, bruises, knife wounds just created layers of more mental toughness in me. There was no compassion or empathy. I was just told to deal with it and shut up. On the way to school each day, it wasn't unusual to see somebody being stabbed or hear about a body from the night before that was shot, lying in a pool of blood in the street. I would be scared and think, "What's going on in this neighborhood?" I was always on guard, ready to be jumped. During seventh grade, I spent a week in the hospital with gut pain caused by a two-inch deep duodenal ulcer. I was driven to this sickness by the worry I faced on a daily basis, and now I had a two-inch gash in my stomach and couldn't eat anything. My friends in the neighborhood thought I was acting. In later years at a class reunion, the women always outnumbered the men, because over fifty percent of the men were either dead through crime or were currently in prison.

I went to Catholic grammar school and public high school. I can remember being in grammar school and being jumped by a number of kids and getting pretty well beaten up. When I got home, my father saw that I had taken a beating and said, "What's going on?" I told him what had happened. Because he was six feet five and 275 lbs. of rock, I really didn't want to. But he was going to get the information out of me no matter what.

Charlestown had an unwritten law, the 'Code of Silence.' If you see anything, you didn't say anything. Listen to a Townie bank robber doing life in prison describe the code: "Charlestown's a spirit. Whether you're a citizen or a criminal, there's a spirit of honor, pride and character. If you left and went to prison, when you came back everybody knew who you were; they never forgot you. It's a tight community. Robbing armored cars just seemed natural. It seemed normal not to rat out anyone."

You see, Townie criminals had an advantage over other criminals. The physical isolation and tight-knit city blocks bred a mistrust of outsiders, and lips stayed shut when police or anybody else came around. This is the 'Code of Silence,' but it was really founded and taught in each family household. So here is the direct result of the Code: eighty percent of the forty-nine murders in a span of fifteen years have gone unsolved, even those that were executed in broad daylight with a few eyes watching. The real impact on my life and the association of the 'Code of Silence' was this: my family, and probably many other families, were living under the Code in their own homes. Our parents taught it this way: "Do as I say, not as I do. Keep your mouth shut if you don't like the way things are being run around here, get your own place or, if not, you will get a smack." The suffering was the inner torment of each child as we watched our parents destroy the family household with this concept.

Dad was always saying one thing and doing another. Once while in high school, it took me months to convince Kathy, this girl I liked who was a cheerleader, for a date. I could not believe it when she agreed. I had just gotten my license, and the one thing I needed was the family car, but first I had to ask Dad's permission. I talked to him at dinner a few days beforehand and expressed the importance of being home on time so I could use the car for my date.

Well, the big day came. My plan was to pick up Kathy at her house at six p.m., meet her parents, and then go to the movies on a date. Dad promised to be home at five-thirty, which would give me plenty of time to get to her house. At five-fifteen, the phone on the kitchen wall rang; it was my dad. There was a lot of noise in the background, but I could hear him say, "I am going to be a few minutes late." I thought, "Oh no, here we go; he is drinking with his buddies and he's going to break his promise to me." Time passed, it was five-fifty, and I called Kathy's house to tell her I was waiting for the car and would be late. The time for our date, six p.m., came and went, and at six-thirty, still no Dad, and no call from him. I looked out the window constantly, hoping every car coming up the street was my dad. A few more calls to Kathy's house, and I was getting really embarrassed. All I could think of was that her parents were asking, "What kind of kid is our daughter dating?" The story ended at nine-thirty that night, as my dad stumbled drunk through the door. After the date incident, my mom tried to convince me things would all work out — she could see that I was furious — but even I knew that it did not make any sense to argue with a man who had been drinking all day with his friends.

There were gang fights continually and there was nothing you could do about it. One day, after I got beat up in a bad gang fight, my dad asked me who the gang leader was. Once Dad got the last name, he realized the gang leader was the son of one of his friends. So I found myself after dinner that same night at the Boy's Club, me and the gang leader, in the boxing ring with the gloves on, to settle it. We punched each other out to a badly fought draw. My dad set it up and later we actually became friends because of it.

We thought we could get away with anything we wanted, even if someone saw what we were doing. I took that with me for a long time. In fact, I can remember during my freshman year playing baseball at Massachusetts Bay Community College, I convinced a few team members that after curfew we could go back to the club by hot wiring the coach's car. Well, that's what we did, and upon returning at three a.m., I got caught red-handed by the coach and paid dearly for it in practice the next day.

I learned from Charlestown to always be aware of the people around me, to be constantly looking over my shoulder. Everybody knew everybody. If a stranger came into the neighborhood, he was interrogated and asked, "What are you doing here? Who are you going to see? Why are you seeing him? How do you know him? What do you want from him?" That's how it was in that day. Everybody was protecting everybody.

When I graduated from high school, my mother's seven brothers were all dockworkers except one, and they assumed I would work on the docks with them. I felt I was on the verge of big trouble, and as soon as I could, I had to get out of Charlestown. I was the first of all my cousins to get married, even though I was not the oldest. I was the first to get out of the 'Town' and the first to start a business. So I packed a duffel bag and left town the summer of 1974. I got married to my wife Barbara in January 1975, and we moved to Waltham, ten miles west. Waltham is more of a suburb, with all different denominations of faith, more middle class, and definitely more peaceful.

I was headed down the wrong road, a bad attitude, horrific language, and a drinking problem. In those days, I believed that what was best for me was best for everyone else. My wife Barbara will tell you that, at times, she was ready to pack it in. I was not easy to live with!

When I told my friends I was going to start a business, they said, "No you're not, you are staying here with us in Charlestown." I was considered a traitor for leaving the 'Town.' People were trying to draw me back in, instead of allowing me to branch out and better myself. They never wanted anyone to improve, to be better than them. When I started to be successful in business, my whole collection of friends changed, and most of my old friends rejected me, and I just never wanted to go back there. I knew I had responsibilities; I was now married, working on building a family. I had just put all my life savings into a new business. I wasn't going to allow myself to be pulled into that trap where I could hurt myself or my family. If I stayed, I would be working the docks and living a life of crime. I knew that drinking, lying and gambling would be major parts of my life. It was a joke that you would have a new pair of sneakers, and a new radio, or TV in the house, but it came off the docks. In a way, my surroundings were teaching me how to steal, lie and cheat.

I cannot close out this chapter without speaking about the good people of Charlestown. The best example is my friend O.C.'s dad, Jack. He helped everyone he met. In fact, he was a fixture at all Charlestown youth hockey and Boston University hockey games. Here is what O.C. said about his dad, "He loved Boston and he could talk about Boston and Charlestown for hours on end. He was part of America's 'Greatest Generation,' a generation of men and women who never asked, 'Why me?' They asked 'Why not me?' They never made excuses; they made decisions and they marched forward. They lived life not with their hand out looking for something from someone, but with their hand extended offering assistance to others. They were servants and their mantra was, 'How can I help? What can I do for you?' And they accepted the accountability of their actions. They believed in God, they believed in America and they paid it forward." There were many like him but this was a special man who I looked up to. Both he and my dad were Korean War veterans and I respected them for that.

After my conversion, which I will talk about in Chapter Three, I learned that I did not have to prove myself to anyone but God, that if I focus on Him, everything else will fall into place. One thing I learned by combining my Charlestown understanding with my conversion is to always seek the truth. Be persistent, be persistent and be persistent. I could work harder than anybody I have met; no one was going to outwork me.

When I look back at my upbringing, first of all, being born and raised in that Charlestown environment had a big influence on me, but I also had faith given to me by my parents. Even though I fell away and didn't practice it as much as I should have, I still had that gift of faith; the gift was engrained in me. We all have that gift through the Sacrament of Baptism and so it's just a matter of revealing it, getting it out into our everyday lives. Those days were frightful, but looking back, I would not trade them for any four-year college degree in the country. I wouldn't change a thing. God had a special plan, and I had no idea what was to come next.

Chapter One Bottom Line

First Gift of the Holy Spirit is Wisdom

Each one of us, young or old can reflect on our history: our family, where we lived and went to school, the jobs we kept. We must ask ourselves, "Why are we living in this time in history?" When I started to look back on my life, I could sense God filling me with wisdom, and preparing me for something by an accumulation of my life experiences. I realized that on any given day, I could have been arrested or killed, but God continually protected me. You're not defined in life by your past experiences, but by your destination. I thank my parents for the gift of my faith, and I would not trade my youth growing up in our home in Charlestown for anything. Everybody has a family history and must grow up somewhere, get over the wounds from the past and do what is right; seek the truth first. The truth is far more powerful than anything else.

This was my true destination.

Wisdom is the first and highest gift of the Holy Spirit, because it is the perfection of the theological virtue of faith. Through wisdom, we come to value properly those things which we believe through faith. The truths of Christian belief are more important than the things of this world, and wisdom helps us to order our relationship to the created world properly, loving Creation for the sake of God, rather than for its own sake.

Source:
http://catholicism.about.com/od/beliefsteachings/p/Faith.htm

Chapter 2

Trying to Impress People

What causes a man to get married two months after his twentieth birthday?

First, I wanted to stay out of Charlestown and out of trouble, and second, there was the awesome Barbara Rossi.

I met my wife Barbara at Massachusetts Bay Community College in Watertown in the fall of 1972, where I was a catcher for our college baseball team. I can remember the day I saw this tall, beautiful woman who was talking with the guys in the back of class about the back-up goalie of the Boston Bruins. I thought to myself, "I have to meet this woman." She had graduated from twelve years of Catholic school in 1971, and was a strong female athlete. Barbara had many favorite sports but she could really shoot the eyes out of a basket in basketball. She could stand at the foul line and just keep making one basket after the next. I saw her talent as a betting edge with my baseball teammates at college. So, to prepare the sting, I would always keep a basketball in the car, just in case some prideful teammates came along for lunch. On the way to lunch we would always stop at a basketball court for a game of twenty-one, to see who was paying for lunch. Once she got the ball in her hand, it was all over and I would win my lunch bet each time.

I really do not know what she saw in me, but I can tell you that we have just celebrated our fortieth wedding anniversary. Her comment about forty years of marriage to me is, "It has been the best twenty years of my life!" I asked her to marry me on our second date, and she was so shocked that she dropped all her books in the street on

Palfrey Hill as I was taking her home from class.

Barbara knows almost everything about sports. In fact, on our thirtieth wedding anniversary, she had a special request: to go to Philly for the Army and Navy football game. For her, it brought back memories of watching this game with her dad, who was a World War II Army veteran. We have attended Super Bowls, World Series, Ryder Cups and many other top sporting events together, and each time, she blows me away with her knowledge of sports. I can remember being in Houston for the second Patriots Super Bowl victory and we decided to get a coffee on our way home. As we were in line, she struck up a conversation with a stranger, and I was thinking, "Who is this guy?" It turns out it was Peter King, the head football writer for *Sports Illustrated*. They talked for half an hour about the Patriots' defense in the upcoming game.

But the real key to my relationship with Barbara is this: I would be nowhere in my life without her. She could have left me at any time, and she certainly deserved better treatment than the way I treated her during the years I was living in the fast lane. I never wanted to disappoint her, even though there were many, many times through my excessive drinking, gambling and lying that I let her down.

In fact, during 1982, it got so bad that I stayed out all night with friends and, as I lay down at home, I began getting chest pains and was carted out in an ambulance to the emergency room. To this day, this episode has remained in our son Jeff's mind as a really bad memory of his dad. I wish I could take those events back and had acted differently.

In those days, I really never read Scripture, but Saint Paul says, "What I do, I do not understand. For I do not DO what I want, but I DO what I hate." (*Romans 7:15*) Saint Paul accurately describes how I felt inside, but I was acting totally different on the outside. I had to prove to everyone that I could succeed, but inside I hated it. In fact, I can remember Barbara asking me one time, "When are you going to stop trying to prove yourself to everybody and just be who you are?" I guess she could see into my heart and knew that I really was not showing on the outside who I was on the inside. It was not until my conversion that I realized she was the best gift from God I could ever have. God put her in my life to keep me grounded and to protect me.

Barbara's a great mother; she's done everything for our two children, Jeff and Nicole. She's helped me with the business and has been supportive of every good thing I did. She built this family to be what it is today. While everyone flocked to Barbara, most people who know me well would say, "Whatever Andy LaVallee did, he did it 1000 percent," and for that I think she's a little bit concerned about how I could change that dramatically and surrender to God's will.

A few years after we got married, I got a call from Barbara saying that she was pregnant with our first child; I started thinking of being a good provider and protector as a father and a husband. I could do the protecting pretty well, but I needed to get serious about the providing part.

Here is what Barbara's brother Victor Rossi said about me:

"For some forty-plus years, I have known Andy LaVallee. We first met when my sister Barbara brought him home to meet the family. They met at college and immediately connected because of their love of sports, especially for the Boston teams. For as long as I can remember, Andy has been driven and determined. You could see that very early on in his career that he knew what he wanted. Yet being one of two of my sister's older brothers, I had my concerns early on. Let's face it, you would have concerns too if your sister was dating a guy that managed to drive his car into a tree going up the steepest street in Watertown, and the weather had nothing to do with it. That's just a small sample of Andy's debut as the future husband of my sister. I'm sure that this life story of Andy's will bring out many of those situations, good and bad, that have molded the person that Andy is today.

"But let's go back to "drive and determination." I always admired his penchant to go for it no matter what. Once his mind is made up, don't even try to sway his decision. In his early years, as a businessman, he would do whatever was necessary to grow his business. The competition was the enemy and he would target their best customers and convince them that he had the better product, service and price. That tactical approach, I'm sure, generated quite a few enemies but it worked. He was never one to take failure lightly. Today he has one of the best small business distributorships in the New England area.

"Now take that "drive and determination" and apply it to golf and horse racing. I didn't just pull these two sports out of the air. Andy, in his younger years, enjoyed gambling and betting on horses. But that alone wasn't good enough. He decides to team up with a couple of friends, hire a trainer and purchase a couple of horses. I'm sure someone probably challenged him to do it and, as always, he accepted the challenge. To the best of my knowledge, that endeavor, although only lasting a few years, again worked out very well. From horse racing to golf and again, let's enter the term "drive and determination." He was told that he could never be granted membership at Charles River Country Club. He didn't fit in socially with its elite membership. Well, another challenge met and still very active some twenty-five years later. He was also told by another member that he didn't have the skills to be a competitive golfer. Not only did he become competitive within the membership, he also qualified for several state amateur tournaments.

"So here we are some forty years later, a devoted husband and family man, who is successful in business and golf, to name a few. But that was not enough for Andy. He also has taken on a new and somewhat controversial challenge, devoting the remainder of his life serving GOD. Yes, controversial because what other subject draws such universal debate around the world? Wars were started centuries ago and remain ongoing over religion. Andy, of course, with the same "drive and determination," has again accepted this mammoth challenge with open arms, never one to do things lightly. He believes that this is his calling in life and he will without any doubt in my mind continue to give it all he has until his last breath. I remain a believer in God and God is extremely lucky to have Andy LaVallee as a member of his team."

I was determined to succeed in areas that no one else from my crowd had tried. So in early 1977, I bought a station wagon for 400 bucks and started to deliver bread on the way home from my night shift at the bakery. I thought I would do this on the side just to make more money with the baby coming, but I quickly learned there was a real need for someone who was going to be reliable at distributing breads. We quickly grew from one customer to twenty accounts doing about $3000 a week in sales. This was enough for me to buy a fourteen-foot box truck and go out on my own as a distributor. I worked seven days a week for seven straight years. I might have been hurt, sick or injured, but never missed one day.

In the first year of the business, we got the largest snow storm in the history of Boston. It was the blizzard of '78, with hurricane winds and four feet of snow. The roads were closed for weeks, but I still found a way to fill up my truck with bread and sell it on the streets of Boston. People would pay anything for a loaf of bread in those catastrophic storm conditions.

I will always be indebted to Albert Quinzani who owned the bakery I was working at when Dad died. He had the confidence in me to extend credit terms, allowed me to work two jobs, and helped me to grow this business. He was one of two men that I did not ever want to disappoint.

The other was Lou Nocera, who owned The Chateau Restaurant in Waltham, a tough no-nonsense businessman who supported every charity in the Waltham area. The Chateau Restaurant in Waltham was one of the highest volume family restaurants around in the late 70's, and they had a reputation for great bread. Although they bought hundreds of loaves of bread daily elsewhere, Lou allowed me to deliver just ten loaves of bread a day, seven days a week. This sure didn't seem like much, but it was an opportunity and an opening to create a relationship by which I might convince him that we could service the entire business.

After a few months, Lou decided that it was time for his customers to decide who had the best bread. My competitor would bring his breads for one month. I would bring my breads for the following month and then he and his customers would make a decision. I offered to take the second month, with the idea that after a full month, we would win the business. I convinced Mr. Quinzani to make the Chateau bread twice a day, for lunch and then again for dinner, and we delivered it hot to the restaurant twice a day. On the first delivery, Lou joined me as we picked up 300 steaming hot loaves of bread, and we needed a towel to wipe the windshield because it was ten degrees outside and all the windows were fogged up, and we couldn't see where we were going. There was no turning back. To this day, we are the main supplier, making Chateau bread on a daily basis.

Today the Chateau Restaurant Group is managed by Lou's son Joe and nothing has changed, except they have grown tremendously. They are still one of our top accounts. In 2006, the Nocera family was inducted in the New England Restaurant Hall of Fame, and they gave my family the unique privilege of introducing them to over 700 people attending this gala dinner. Both families sat together with three generations of entrepreneurs talking family business, as we found out that we were the first vendor in the history of the event to introduce a customer to the Hall of Fame. Lou Nocera took a huge risk trusting in a twenty-three-year-old kid back then, and I know in my heart today that our business might not have survived without the continued loyalty and support of the Nocera family.

We started the business in 1977 and, for many years, it was a pretty stable business, growing each year. I went from one truck to two trucks, from sixty accounts to 120 accounts. We were still just this home-based business with an office in my basement and two trucks parked at a gas station. We had no facility or building. You might have called us a "jobber" back then. One of the ways I was able to build the business is through the drive I have because of what happened between me and my dad. I told myself, "I'm going to do this and nothing's going to stop me."

As I said earlier, it took working seven days a week for seven straight years to build this business, and I never missed one day. I'd wake up at ten p.m., collect all the orders off the answering machine, and then I would put them on the paperwork. I'd drive my car to the bakery, pick up the truck, pick up the different supplies at different bakeries, make the deliveries throughout the night, go home at eight or nine in the morning, take a shower and get dressed. Then I would go out in the daytime, create new accounts, sell clients, go back to bed at two or three in the afternoon, then get up again at ten p.m. I did that every day for years.

I missed a lot of our family's life, but thank God for Barbara. She was there raising the kids while I was the provider; we were actually a pretty traditional family. She was on board, assisting me if something went wrong. For example, if a truck broke down on the road, she'd pile the kids in the car, and she'd meet me and take me to get a truck rental. She was always there for me. She did the paperwork: all the statements and all the invoices. This was before computers so it was all handwritten.

With our success in the bread business, we were able to put our two children through college. Jeff was a business major and graduated from Lehigh, and Nicole was a dance major and graduated from Dean College in Franklin, Massachusetts. They are both talented in different ways and are both partners in the family business.

I've always been very relationship-driven from the beginning. I was able to learn Greek to relate to my customers and show respect for their culture. I could actually take orders in the Greek language. It was a great start, but soon our business would go international.

In the spring of 2001, Charlie Fox, a friend of mine, was at a bar in Boston, and he met this guy from a bakery in Montreal called Au Pain Dore. It is owned by Jean-Marc

Etienne and family, with a pretty similar make-up to us: he had two adult children in his business. Over a few drinks, his sales rep Michel and Charlie got talking. Michel had just come to Boston to find a distributor to bring their product to the United States. They were there for a whole week, met with many distributors, but nobody wanted to give them a shot. So Charlie gave them my card. A few weeks later, I found myself in Montreal, looking at this facility and saying to myself, "This is world class." It was great for both of us. Jean-Marc got a salesman with a bakery background, and we got an exceptional product for our customers.

My wife and I had planned to go to the Master's Tournament in Augusta, Georgia. James Driscoll, a young man who grew up at our golf club, had qualified through his runner-up finish in the U.S. amateur and was playing in the Masters, an incredible honor. So I had them ship the bread to Augusta to test its durability and quality. Every morning, the FedEx truck would show up at Driscoll's house and we would test the bread. I was thinking, "This is incredible, it was baked yesterday and this was the best bread I had ever tasted," and all the other houseguests agreed. So as I was walking the green fairways of Augusta, I said to myself, "This is the next generation of bread and we must go there. Don't blow it, big guy!" But their impression of me was that I was this big distributor out of Boston, with a huge facility, and I did nothing to change that.

To get started with Au Pain Dore, we rented an offsite twenty-by-twenty freezer and when the trailer came down from Montreal, we'd squeeze 150 cases in the freezer and then we'd sell it, then we'd put another 150 cases in and sell it. So each time Jean-Marc came to Boston, we were introducing him to the new clients we had, but he wanted to see our facility. I would always take him to more customers, so we finally cut this deal between us that Au Pain Dore would give us this exclusivity with the breads in the USA. One night he came to Boston. We went to dinner and had a few bottles of wine and he said, "Can I finally see your facility?" I replied, "Sure, come on, let's go."

So I took him to my home, to the basement office in my house — which at the time was my entire facility — and placed all the orders for the night, handed off the invoices and paperwork to my driver who was coming and we went out. Jean-Marc was shaking his head and was probably thinking, "What did I get into here?! This is not the distributor I thought we partnered with. How did I miss this?"

The second year we sold just below 40,000 cases. The third year we cracked a million dollars in sales. We made the commitment to expand the business from a home business to a full scale business with warehouse, freezer, new trucks and office, along with everything else. We were now branding ourselves as "The Bakery Specialist."

We currently have 24,000 square feet and we have grown from having three vendors regionally to over twenty-eight vendors internationally. Our product mix now has cookies, croissants, wraps and baguettes, each product the customer needs for all of his four segments: breakfast, lunch, dinner, catering and institution. Our clients today are The Boston Red Sox, The InterContinental, the Four Seasons, Ritz Carlton, Boston Harbor Hotel, Boston College, Boston University, Gillette Stadium and the Chateau Restaurant Group and so many other great customers.

Back in 1979, after we founded LaVallee Bakery Distributors and it started to become successful, I was beginning to think of another venture, something in which very few people are successful. I had been hanging out at the racetrack after delivering bread, and accumulating some gambling winnings through my connections. I started to think of owning my own thoroughbred racehorses where I could make some real money and I actually bought a horse. The statistics show that eighty percent of horse owners lose money. So it was my intention to find out why and outwork everyone to get into the twenty percent category that made money. Besides, I couldn't afford to make one mistake or I would be out of business.

It didn't take long to get hooked. My first win was in Philadelphia at Keystone Racetrack. Even though I was only in the business about a month, I knew this horse was ready and I wanted to make a score. After delivering bread all night, I went home, showered and raced to Logan Airport to get a flight to Philly. After taking a cab out to the track and meeting my trainer in the paddock, I bet two hundred to win for the jockey, and our horse won pretty easily. We made a $9,500 score. After a few beers, I flew back to Boston that night, didn't go to bed, got right in the truck to deliver bread and went back to work. I was making a nickel for each roll I delivered after working all night long. I might make a profit of $70 or $80. I was juggling two businesses, working odd hours and really taking a big risk drinking and driving home late at night. I thought I was bulletproof.

In fact, I can remember driving my car late into the morning hours, probably having had too much to drink. The passenger in my car was a person I grew up with, but someone I didn't know all that well. Most kids from the neighborhood would keep a nightstick or a set of brass knuckles under the front seat, not the knucklehead I was with, and at the spur of the moment, he decided to empty his revolver into the sky out the passenger side window of my car. Only God knows why we did not get killed!

I think after my dad died, I spent a lot of time trying to impress people, but I did not realize until later they were all the wrong people. I was trying to show everyone that I was going to survive, to adjust without my dad. The racetrack was a perfect place to do just that. I was trying to impress upon people the idea, "I can do this" because my dad was always a fear motivator saying, "You're never going to be able to do this, you can't do this. You're not good enough for this," and that kind of thing. I had that burning desire to show everybody he was wrong, but I was showing all the wrong people.

I was willing to do anything to accomplish this goal; it even brought me to crime. I cannot say at this point I even considered whether my actions were sinful or had any effect on my soul. I would compromise anything to make a buck. I couldn't sleep at night, because I was embarrassed at what I had become. You needed serious money to play in this game, money that I did not have. One of the things I am most ashamed of is when I took money from my family to fund my gambling habits. I pray that they forgive me and that I can repay them someday.

At this point, there was not much I had not gambled on: sports, cards, casino black jack and craps. For me it was always a war; they wanted my money and I wanted theirs. Once in April of 1985, my friend and I took out a home improvement loan to go to Vegas. We planned to postpone construction, take the money to Las Vegas and bet the money on our home fighter. In the remarkable fight, Marvin Hagler beat Tommy Hearns. The fight went down in boxing history as one with the most punches recorded in eight minutes. Hagler turned it into a street fight and knocked out the Detroit boxer with the nickname 'hit man' in the third round. We won a bundle of cash and paid off the loan on our return home from Vegas and kept the profit. These are the type of risks we took.

At the track, everyone was out to beat you: the owners, the trainers, the jockeys, and even the gate crew would fix a race to bring in some cash. Did you ever see a race when one horse gets a very late start? Well, that's because the gate crew tied his tail to the gate and it took a few seconds to untangle, just enough to take that horse out of the race. The perfect scenario is when you have two or three groups all working to fix the same race, and then you could get a real price for your horse. My stable was mostly right in the thick of things. It got to the point where we started to win pretty consistently, and the wiseguys started to take notice.

In early 1980, I owned eleven thoroughbred racehorses. We had won twenty-seven races the year before and made enough money from our winnings to buy a house. Yes, a house, not another horse! One of the older guys at the track turned to me one day. "Hey kid, you just made a fine score, why don't you buy your family a nice house?" So I took $30,000 of my winnings and we bought a beautiful ninety-foot ranch home in Waltham. This was great advice, since Barbara and I were living in an apartment, paying $175 month for rent when I owned hundreds of thousands of dollars worth of horses.

With this lifestyle, there was a lot of drinking going on and many women were interested in getting attached to someone with money, so I was always living on the edge. I often asked myself in secret, "What price am I willing to pay for all this?" I remember making so much money one weekend that we flew to New York for the weekend to bet the races at Aqueduct, and then drove through the Lincoln Tunnel to the Meadowlands at night. My wife was getting sick and tired of it, and started to lay down the law. Looking back, I cannot blame her.

We owned a world class horse that was probably one of the best horses in New England at the time. His name was Irish Lament. When we bought him, he was a bad stall walker. That means that when he entered the stall, he would walk in circles continuously. So we found a way to put Plexiglas mirrors in the stall and he stopped walking, put on weight, trained like a thoroughbred and ran like a champion. We entered him into a Saturday feature race with a $35,000 purse. He was a cinch; no one could beat him. He had just won four in a row when I was approached by the wiseguys who said, "Hey, we need to do business. You're not going to win this race." I had been connected with the wiseguys for a while, and always played ball, but this was a huge purse. What mattered most to me was that it was my horse, and if I won, it would move me to the next level. I was not interested in this exchange. I knew we were a heavy favorite and could win. I refused the deal, and the next day we had visitors at the barn that caused me to scratch the horse out of the race.

This is when I said, "Okay. I'm done and I'm out of here. If I am not careful, I will end up with all my classmates in jail." My guardian angel was really working overtime in those days; I had been in the racehorse business for four years. So I got up one morning and decided to sell all of my horses. It was part of my life but I wasn't proud of it. I walked away and never looked back.

All my life, I was involved in sports. I played Babe Ruth baseball, high school baseball and basketball, along with a year of college baseball before I quit school. I needed to find something that was going to keep me motivated, help me stay active, challenge me and, most of all, keep me out of trouble. So I decided to take up golf. In early 1985 as member of the Waltham Lions Club, I met and befriended champion blind golfer Joe Lazaro. Joe had been a state champion high school golfer and who stepped on a land mine in World War II and lost his sight entirely. He had just won seven national blind championships and could break eighty blind. When he received the Ben Hogan Award at the National Golf Writers' Dinner in 1970, he challenged Sam Snead to a golf match. He told Snead, "You pick the course and I will pick the time — midnight." My thoughts were if Joe, being blind, could play golf, then I would be able to play. One problem was that all I knew about golf was when we stole golf clubs out of the cars in Charlestown. Eventually, Joe Lazaro was responsible for sponsoring my family into Charles River Country Club in 1991. I sometimes wonder what my two kids would be like if they had been brought up at the racetrack rather than the golf course.

When we became members of the Charles River Country Club in Newton, Massachusetts, I was again motivated to improve my golf game to impress all those guys who laughed at me. Both of my kids, Jeff and Nicole, loved it at the Club; the pool, golf and all snacks were charged to Dad's number. I met friends that were very successful in corporate and business life with private jets and expense accounts that brought me a long way from the racing world. I was respected by my friends at the Club because I had come from the Town, a background they were very familiar with. Most people knew the Charlestown reputation and, for them, I was an underdog.

At this time, I was going to Sunday Mass occasionally, not really going to confession, living by my own rules. I was not part of a parish; I wanted to be the visitor, under the radar screen, in and out as quickly as possible. If it was a Sunday and I planned to play golf, I might not go to Mass or, if I went to Mass, I snuck out of the pew early to get to the parking lot as quickly as I could after receiving the Eucharist so that I would be on the first tee. I was in the car five seconds after Communion. It was very disrespectful.

Golf became my god. I committed all my spare time to be a better golfer. It was another challenge. I started with a twenty-five handicap and I wanted to be a golfer who could compete in state events. If you take all the golfers in the country, two to three percent have a handicap of three or less, and I accomplished that in eight years.

My practice schedule and playing rounds were intense. One year I played 265 rounds of golf. I charted out my practice time in order to identify what my needs were, and spent time in each area of improving my game. In my first year, I took a four-day rules seminar at The U.S.G.A., and later found out I was the only non-professional in the class. My score was 78 on the 100 question test; not bad for an amateur trying to learn the game. I hired the best teaching coaches I could find, and played four to five rounds per week, practicing twenty hours more per week. The real secret was the putting. I practiced every night making fifty consecutive four-foot putts in a row. If I missed one, I started all over. Because of this drill, putting became my reputation. If you can putt, you can play with anybody. For you golfers reading this, I know you're thinking, "To make fifty putts will take all day." Not really. Once you get in a zone and turn this over to the subconscious, you can accomplish it in about forty minutes.

The competition and gamesmanship in golf captured me entirely. It was right up my alley, and I even enjoyed my time in the grill room, having a few pints after golf. Charles River was a very competitive club with many scratch golfers, and even more scratch drinkers. Most members were self-employed businessmen who wanted to use the facility to enjoy themselves after work. I was an instigator when it came to this fellowship, and I love the guys with whom I spent time discussing all the problems of the world. My time in the grill room would start with just a cold pint or two at the end the day, and then next thing I knew I had ten or twelve pints and was headed for trouble. The evil one had me wrapped around his finger, and I was starting to be a star player for the wrong team. For those of you who do not believe there is a devil, I am telling you firsthand that he is real. He would convince me "just one more," and I fell for it each time, trying to figure out how I got stuck down this road.

I applied the same work ethic to golf that I did to my business; find a mentor, find the best people around me that I could learn from and work harder than anybody else. Basically that's all I was trying to do. In 1999, I qualified for the state amateur and mid-amateur with scores of seventy-four. A qualifier was among about 120 players trying to achieve one of the top six spots to go to the state level competition. It was very competitive and a grind, but that year our club set a U.S.G.A. record by filling all four regional spots for the prestigious U.S. Amateur Championship. My success in golf gave me the opportunity to travel all over the world and play on some of the best golf courses. It wasn't all play. However, the business grew thirty-five percent that first year while I was playing golf.

Golf was very important to me. I wanted to be around the best people, the best players, and I look back at these experiences and I think, "These are the experiences which God put in front of me for this moment right now." It's important to be around the right people now, the people who understand what I am doing and who communicate in a certain way. It was a similar type of journey as my conversion. However, the result is totally different. It takes time, it takes patience and it takes work to achieve any goal you have in life.

Barbara and I established lifelong friendships with many of these fellow members, and I am thankful to them for all they did for our family and our children. Our son Jeff caddied and played junior golf at Charles River C.C. throughout his high school years. He applied under early decision to Lehigh University in order to play on the golf team. When he got a deferral letter, he was very upset. However, the Friday after Thanksgiving, he caddied for a member who knew a benefactor who had just donated $25,000,000 to the school. All it took was for these two to spend four hours on the golf course and a phone call from the member to the benefactor, and a week later, Jeff was accepted to his dream college to play golf. Another great story about the generosity of these people was in the fall of 2009 when our daughter Nicole got married. A few of Barbara's girlfriends at the club loved Nicole so much they gave her an incredible wedding gift: a trip to Hawaii! Let me tell you, there were great people in Charlestown but no one with the ability to match this.

In 1995, one of my son's high school coaches became very sick with cancer. They held a prayer service in a parish in South Waltham. It was not my parish, but I was so impressed with the priest's homily that I started making it my regular parish. After a year, in 1996, the priest asked me to teach religious education, or C.C.D. (Confraternity of Christian Doctrine) He said, "Just do it for one year." It was high school sophomore and freshman boys, a Confirmation Class. I taught it for thirteen years. What I was doing was learning the Catechism from a perspective I was never taught; there was a little bit of an appetite there. But I was living as a hypocrite because I was teaching Catholicism, but not living it; it was such a divided life. I was able to give the boys real life examples of faith, because I was looking at people from the perspective of saints. Many young men were without sponsors for Confirmation, so I would fill the void left by unsupportive family members in their lives. I had a good rapport with the boys. I am in touch with some of them to this day.

We have a young man working in our facility now who was part of one of those first classes. My C.C.D. Director told me that I really should watch over this guy, Marcus, because he had a violent temper. My response was, "Yeah, whatever, I am not worried about this kid. He's a freshman in high school." The news came out that he was not in class this particular night, and I found out that it was because he had gotten into a fist fight with the principal of the high school and they had arrested him. Sounds like somebody I know. So he came to C.C.D. the following week, and he was playing with some money on his desk. I told him to put it away and he didn't. I told him two more times and he still refused. I took the money out of his hand, and I tore it up into 100 pieces, and put it into this envelope. I handed it back to him and said, "Now when you get home, you can play with this all you want, and tape it all back together like a big puzzle, but in this class you won't fool around anymore." That's when Marcus got up from behind his desk, picked it up and threw it at me. We got into an altercation and the way I handled it was, a week later, he was going to come and apologize to me in front of the class. He did, and then I gave him a job at the LaVallee Bakery. We got him in some classes with Dale Carnegie through my friend John MacKinnon, who was the owner. Marcus attended anger management classes, and as a senior in high school, he became the Senior Class President. Now he is our warehouse manager on our night shift. At graduation, I stood next to Marcus' mom and she was so proud that he was staying out of trouble. She reminded me of my own mom.

My mom, like my dad, also drank regularly. On the third floor of our triple-decker, my bedroom was about ten by five feet, with no closet. The next room over was my mom and dad's bedroom. One day when I was a junior in high school, Dad was off with his buddies somewhere in mid-afternoon while my mother was drinking and I was studying in my room. All of a sudden, I smelled smoke. She had been smoking a cigarette, fell asleep on the bed and set the bed on fire. So here I was on the third floor, a teenager, wondering, "How do I save her and the house?" That was the kind of stuff that happened to me.

So when Dad died, I was going to take over the family. It was a bad decision because my brothers didn't want me to tell them what to do, and that's why Barbara and I got married so young. It was like, 'Let's get out of here. Let's start this thing over again.'

My mom had seven brothers who were constantly keeping an eye on me. She was always protecting me by not telling my father about all the stuff I was involved with. She was a true stay-at-home mom. I loved Mom dearly, but I was drawn to my Dad.

In early June 1983, I got a call around five in the morning from my brother Arty. He had just returned from a night out with his buddies to find my mother dead on the floor from a heart attack. It had been almost eight years since Dad died; now it was happening all over again. I really miss her love and kindness, and I was soon to find out how much a man needs the influence of his mother.

Chapter Two Bottom Line

Second Gift of the Holy Spirit is Understanding

To relive the events of these past two chapters was difficult for me: it brought back many painful memories of the people I hurt. I had a hard time trying to understand all the things I did. The real lesson I learned is, "Who are you trying to prove yourself to?"

Love and respect those around you. The only one you have to impress is God Himself. If we could only see ourselves as God sees us, that's the real understanding! Everything else is transitory; nothing material in this world is worth a thing. It took me years of pain and suffering to figure this out.

Surrender everything to God's plan for you, not your plan for you, and it will all fall in place. I was soon to learn I had to put Him first in all things.

Understanding is the second gift of the Holy Spirit, and people sometimes have a hard time understanding (no pun intended) how it differs from wisdom. While wisdom is the desire to contemplate the things of God, understanding allows us grasp, at least in a limited way, the very essence of the truths of the Catholic Faith. Through understanding, we gain a certitude about our beliefs that moves beyond faith.

Source:
http://catholicism.about.com/od/beliefsteachings/p/Understanding.htm

Chapter 3
A Mother's Love

"Andrew, Andrew," my mom called out, as I raced down the stairs from my room to the front door on the way to school. "Please pray a Hail Mary to the Blessed Mother today, if not for you, then for me." My parents always called me Andrew when something was important. That was my mom, always watching out for me.

I remember her deep devotion to the Blessed Mother and to the Infant of Prague. As an eighth grader, I always took Mom's advice. I had to walk past this huge statue of the Blessed Mother that was directly across the street from Saint Francis De Sales Church, to and from school each day. I thought it was crazy but I did it for my mom, and besides, it was a violent time in our neighborhood, and I could use all the protection I could get.

Fast forward to the spring of 2010. I was going to Sunday Mass pretty regularly. I had been teaching C.C.D. for boys for ten years at Saint Charles in Waltham, for Father Copp, but he would be really terrified if he knew the kind of life I was living as I was teaching the boys about the Holy Spirit, the Sacraments and the saints! I was going to Mass but, as I learned later, I was not receiving the Holy Eucharist in state of grace. Still, there were times as a C.C.D. teacher that I felt I was 'in the zone.' I would go into class, without notes prepared, and stuff would just flow and it would be a great class. So here I was, considering attending the Boston Catholic Men's Conference, but since I had never gone to conferences or retreats, I was unsure whether I should go. My friend Joe said, "You should go, and bring your son Jeff."

So we went to the conference, and the keynote speaker

was Jim Caviezel. At the time, I hadn't seen *The Passion of the Christ*, so I had no idea who Jim was. He opened up his talk saying, "I always love coming to Boston because of the 1980 Olympic Hockey Team beating the big, bad Russians. They taught me to believe in miracles. Most of those players were from Boston. I keep telling my agent, 'I'd love to meet those guys.' I don't know what it is, but he's never put me in touch with them." So he continued with his talk, and I was saying to myself, "He wants to meet those guys; I grew up with the best one!" Jack O'Callahan (O.C.) and I had been friends for fifty years; we grew up a few blocks from each other. So I gave my card to one of the event organizers, and next thing I knew, the conference ended and I was sitting at a table with Jim Caviezel, Cardinal Sean O'Malley and my son Jeff. Jim was asking me questions about the guys on the Olympic Hockey Team. He told me that when he watched the 1980 team, it had a big impact on his life and career.

Then he said, "By the way, you have to come to Medjugorje with me this summer." I responded, "Hey, Jim, I have no idea what Medjugorje is." Then I looked over and Tim Van Damm was standing a few feet away. He was Jim's assistant during that weekend. Jim was with his wife Kerry for that whole weekend as he spoke to the Men's Conference; she addressed the Women's Conference. So Jim repeated, "You're coming to Medjugorje with me this summer!" I replied, "Look, Jim, don't get your hopes up, because I'm not flying fifteen hours to pray a Rosary!" Looking back and remembering that I said that in front of the Cardinal, it was probably not the best idea! So as we left, Jim said, "We're going to get together; we're going to become friends." I said, "Whatever," and I left thinking, "Can you imagine this guy saying we are going to become friends? He's a movie star in Hollywood, and I'm from Charlestown and he's going to become friends with me? Why would a guy who played Jesus Christ in a big-time movie want to become friends with me?"

The next day, I was getting ready to go to Mass, running a little late, and the cell phone beeped. It was an eight-minute voicemail from Jim Caviezel. I came home and started listening to it. Jim was saying the same thing. "You have to go to Medjugorje, and Kerry's speaking today. Please come to the Women's Conference." I thought, "No way, I'm not going over there." So I played golf instead.

Tim Van Damm, the conference organizer and Caviezel's assistant, soon became a lay spiritual director of mine. Tim was a young go-getting spiritual entrepreneur. He had recently become the catalyst to bring Perpetual Eucharistic Adoration back to the city of Boston for the first time in forty years. Here is how he convinced Father Peter Grover, the director of Saint Clements' Eucharistic Shrine. "We need to re-institute Perpetual Adoration." Father replied, "No way, we're not doing it, you can't get enough people to fill the hours." Tim assured him. "Don't worry, I'll get the people." Father said, "You get the people and I'll consider it."

A month later, he brought Father a chart with all the hours of the week filled with three people in each hour." Tim does not mess around. That's why I love him so much! Then Cardinal O'Malley came to celebrate Holy Mass and launch Perpetual Eucharistic Adoration in Boston. Can you believe that this event made front page in the Boston Globe?!

Tim is so knowledgeable about the Catholic faith. When I met Jim Caviezel and he asked me to come to Medjugorje, I didn't know a thing about Medjugorje; I didn't even know how to spell it! I felt embarrassed that Jim knew about the reported apparitions but I didn't. One thing I did know was my new friend Jim was going to the extreme to get me to go there. Jim and I kept talking, but he was not making any progress. I was still not going to Medjugorje.

Then one day as I was visiting a customer in Everett, the next town over from Charlestown, my car was detoured up Bunker Hill Street, where I lived till I was nineteen. As I was driving up the street, I reflected to myself. "Boy, I have not been here in years." Then my cell phone rang. I tried to answer it, but there was static on the line and was not clear. I started to get a clearer signal, so I pulled over and parked in front of the statue of the Blessed Mother where I prayed as I walked to and from school each day. It was Jim. "Hey, Andy, are we going to Medjugorje in June? It's the last chance for you to come." I looked up and thought, "Wow! I am parked right in front of the statue of the Blessed Mother!" I was a little stunned, so I found myself saying, "Okay. I will be there. When can we meet?" Jim asked, "What changed your mind?" I replied, "I will let you know when I see you in person."

I started thinking, "I don't know what this means, but I guess I am going on a pilgrimage for the first time in my life." I just sensed it. I didn't know what to think, but I felt peace in it. There was something in me which said, 'You better do this.' When that happened to me in my life, it was usually a pretty good sign, yet this was a different feeling. It was not the same business instinct, yet I still felt that I had to listen.

So I called Tim and I said, "Guess what? We're going to Medjugorje!" He asked, "What do you mean we're going to Medjugorje?" I replied, "I just told Caviezel I would go, but I am not going without you." So he said, "Are you asking or telling?" I said, "Telling." He answered, "Okay. I'm in."

In the meantime, I called my friend Jack O'Callahan

from the 1980 Olympic Hockey Team, and I got a poster picture of Jack on his knees with his arms raised in victory as they beat the Russians. A few weeks later, we played golf together and Jack signed the poster to Jim and his whole family. I rolled it up and carried it with me on the flight to Medjugorje. I felt a little more comfortable with Tim there; he had experienced Medjugorje before and was friendly with some of the priest and visionaries.

I found out later this was going to be Caviezel's seventh trip. Here is what he said about being introduced to Medjugorje: "My wife went to Medjugorje while I was in Ireland shooting the movie, *The Count of Monte Cristo*. She started talking about Medjugorje, and how one of visionaries was about to come to Ireland. I interrupted her by saying, 'Listen, I really have some serious work to do. I am not able now to go into anything with any of the visionaries.' Besides that, I thought that, as a Catholic, I didn't have to necessarily accept Lourdes or Fatima or Medjugorje. That is how I thought."

Jim continued. "The visionary Ivan Dragicevic came to Ireland, and I knew straightaway that I would not have time for him, since I had to work all the time. One day, my movie partner Jim Harris wasn't feeling well, so I got the day off and I was able to attend an apparition. I stood at the very back of the packed church, and I wasn't quite sure about what was going on. When the man next to me in his wheelchair fell to his knees at the time of the apparition, I was deeply moved. I thought, 'This handicapped man, despite all of his pains, is kneeling down on the cold stone floor, and he is praying!' Today I realize only God could have known me so well. He knew where exactly He needed to touch me to get my attention! One thing I can tell you, if it were not for Medjugorje, I would never have played Christ in *The Passion*."

On the flight over, I was reading Jan Connell's book *Queen of the Cosmos*. It captivated me so much that I silently contemplated having a life confession in Medjugorje. I started wondering, "Can the Blessed Mother really be appearing there? Come on, is it really true? If it's true, then I have a lot of cleaning up to do!" In the last five years, I had been to confession infrequently, but they were not very good confessions, or even worthy of God's mercy. I was a self-employed businessman filled with pride, and assumed that all the crime, violence and sin throughout my life could not be forgiven. After landing in Dubrovnik, we were in a car headed to Medjugorje and, during the ride, I said to myself, "If the Blessed Mother is really coming from Heaven to earth, then I am not worthy of this. But if I can get in front of God in a sincere confession, maybe there will be a chance. If I am going to be in her presence, this is what I will do." It wasn't like this was a plan; I was just contemplating it.

So the car pulled up to the hotel in Medjugorje and we checked into our rooms. We were staying right next to Ivan's chapel, looking right up a mountain. I asked Tim, "What's that crucifix up there?" He answered, "Oh, that's Cross Mountain, a thirty-foot high white cement crucifix with a relic of the original cross inside it." I said, "Tim, it's two different colors." He asked, "What do you mean?" I replied, "It's blue, white, blue, white." He said, "I don't see blue, white, and blue, white." And then he stopped and said, "Oh wait, now it is blue, white, blue, white." I asked, "Is someone up there filming a movie or something?" He shook his head. "There's nothing up there, no electricity, nothing. Andy, this is a Medjugorje wakeup call." I replied, "Yeah, we'll see." I didn't believe it.

The next day we met with Jim Caviezel. I gave him the picture of Jack O' Callahan and he loved it. Then we walked through the fields in order to go to Mass. It felt really odd, not like the plush fairways I was used to, not even like the busy sidewalks of Boston. I did not tell anybody during the walk, but I was filled with anticipation, and my heart was pounding as we prayed a Rosary together.

We met up with Jim after Holy Mass, and he said, "We're going across the street to Colombo's for brunch. Why don't you guys join us?" First Tim and I walked to Leo's Jewelry Store, a few hundred yards away, to get a four-way medal similar to what Tim was wearing. I had not worn a religious medal since my mom made me wear one years ago. Tim thought it was important so I agreed to get one. We walked up the street to join Jim for lunch and as we approached the table, I saw Jim at a big round table holding court with six priests. Tim and I joined them, and we made it a party of nine. There was delicious-looking Croatian food everywhere; it was like a big feast. One of the priests, Father Michael Lightner, was sitting directly across from me. No lightweight at six feet, four inches, about 330 pounds, Fr. Michael played college and pro football and had worked security for the band U2.

Father Michael was telling everyone at the table about his conversion in Medjugorje. He was all banged up, with bruises and bandages like he got beat up in a bad street fight and I thought, "This guy is full of it." Later I learned that he had just had a bad motorcycle spill. Then the topic switched to his conversion in Medjugorje. In his younger days, his mom Joyce found some drugs in his duffle bag, and was so upset that she forced him to go with her to Medjugorje. When he arrived there, Father Michael challenged God, saying, "If you exist, I do not know You. You got one week to show me who You are. After that, I am out of here!" That one phrase made me believe him and his story. He told us about his life confession and spoke of confessing major sins like alcohol, drugs, pornography and many more. After his confession, he said he felt this pressure pinning him back in the confessional and he thought, "Okay, God, I believe you're real!"

On a return trip to Medjugorje a few months later, he was attending a healing service at Saint James Church, and there was a woman in a wheelchair and he watched as the priest prayed over her. Then he heard a voice come to him. "Michael, I want you to become a priest." He answered, "I don't know who this is, but I'm not doing it." Then the voice said, "If I get her out of this wheelchair, will you enter the seminary?" Father Michael said to this voice, "Have her get up out of the wheelchair and walk around the church, then I'll know it's You."

I was thinking, "*That* takes guts!"

Father Michael continued telling his story. "The priest prayed over her. Then she got out of the wheelchair, walked around the church, came up to me and said, 'Now will you serve the Lord?'" All 330 pounds of this huge man fell to his knees, and he became a priest.

Suddenly, there was a silence at the table. All of us were in awe and I remembered that previous night I had seen a cross in a mountain change colors. Then Father Michael's unbelievable story started me thinking that there might be something special here. Father Michael looked directly at me. "I know you're a friend of Jim's, but what are you doing here, Andy?" I replied, "Father Michael, I really don't know." He said, "For me, when I got away from all that rubbish, it started in confession, and if you haven't been in a while, you might need a life confession."

It was like somebody took a sword and pierced me right

in my heart, like God was saying to me, "I'm asking you to do this *right now*." I said to myself, "Come on, this isn't possible. Can God really be telling me to do this?" Then the Charlestown side of me came out, and this is what was going on in my mind. I looked at the table, there were several bottles of wine and delicious food and the guy who was sitting across from me — he might be a priest but he weighs 330 pounds — and I told myself, "There's no way he's getting up from this table! Look at this stuff, look at the cutlets, he's not leaving this!" So sure in my mind that it was not going to happen, I turned to him. "Father Michael, I just contemplated a life confession on the way here. You might even know that. Let's go do a confession right now." He said, "Okay, let's go." Now I was really convinced I had to do this!

We got up from that beautiful table and went across the street to Saint James' Church. He walked into the sacristy, put on his vestments, got two chairs, then carefully put them closely facing each other as we sat down. He took so much care in placing these chairs that I was starting to ask myself, "Will he pay that much attention to my sins?" Then I began, "Bless me, Father, for I have sinned." He said, "Hold on, this is what we are going to do. You give me your sins by the decade, from 0-10 years, 10-20 years, 20-30 years and so on, each decade that you lived; the things you did, what you were challenged with, thinking about, everything. I want to know everything, don't hold anything back. Give me everything."

So then I start with ages 0-10; I stole some candy bars, beat up my brother and disrespected this one, that one. Then, between ages 10 and 20, I stole some money from my parents' dresser, stole a car, broke into a house. I was getting into some serious sins. I was not holding back. From ages 20 to 30, I laid it all on the line and during ages 40 to

50, he said, "Okay. I get it; here is what's going on. All your sins are sins of abandonment. Has anybody really close to you died in your life?"

I thought, "This is starting to get really scary. He is a mind reader!" So then I told him all about my dad. This went on for two and a half hours and, by the end, I was bawling; my clothes were soaked with my tears. I was exhausted, but I never felt better in my entire life! I didn't need Lufthansa to get home; I could have flown home on my own! So we started to wrap it up when I took the four-way medal out of my pocket that I bought earlier at Leo's, and asked him to bless it and put it on me. So he said "Hold on to it; I am going to give you absolution, I want you to understand some things might happen that you've never experienced before, so don't freak out on me." I didn't know what he meant. So for whatever reason, he wanted to prepare me for what I was about to experience. He said "Bow your head." We were sitting knee to knee, me and this man whom I now felt not only represents God but has direct access to Him. He placed his fist on my chest, he had his other hand on my forehead, and I felt like someone had just turned an iron on, his hand was so hot. He was hitting me in the chest with his fist, praying, "Almighty Father, I pray to You to soften this man's heart." Father was praying to the Lord for me, he was giving me absolution, and I was sitting there with my hands folded. I was listening, saying to myself, "What the heck's going on here?" I was starting to doubt. Then, for the first time in my life, I heard someone speaking in tongues, but when I focused on my heart and God, and trusted, suddenly I heard him speaking in English, loud and clear.

Between the speaking in tongues, and the heat of his hand on my head, I had never experienced anything like this before. We finished the confession. I handed him the medal, and he reached for a black pouch beside him filled with bottles of blessed oil. He then blessed the medal with holy water and holy oils, and placed it around my neck, and it's never been off my neck since then. You could give me a million dollars in cash and I would not take this medal off!

I walked away from confession and I knelt in the stones and dust behind Saint James Church, and prayed my penance of seven hundred seventy Our Fathers, slow and from the heart, just like Father Michael said. I learned a couple of things. Father Michael didn't just give me the Sacrament of Confession. He taught me all the reasons why I was acting out in the sins I was committing. He told me that they were sins of abandonment; I was missing the love of my father, because he abandoned me, not only for the times he left me in the car, or failed to show up at my sporting events, but from his heart attack and death. I really needed him to be there, and he wasn't, and I had to forgive him for that. I had to forgive myself for what I had done to him, because I had carried that with me for thirty-five years. Once I was able to forgive my father, and myself, I would be able to receive the Lord's full mercy and forgiveness for everything I had done. Then, most importantly, when I was given that opportunity to do it for other people, I had to do the same. God was showing me His example of forgiveness through this amazing sacrament, and I needed to embrace this forgiveness. This was going to be the center of my relationship with Our Lord. He was going to teach me the power of love and forgiveness.

I knelt behind Saint James Church, with two hands on the wooden bench for support; I was soaked in perspiration, and it was painful. As I prayed the Our Father, as slowly as I have ever prayed it, I felt the presence of our loving Mother. She was there to comfort me just as she did her Son. Even though I looked like I had just fallen out of a dumpster, and there were many people walking by me, nobody stopped to see if I was all right. To them, it was just another stunning conversion in the miraculous village of Medjugorje.

From the time I left the table at Colombo's, I was gone for almost six hours, so I returned to the hotel afterwards. Tim asked, "What the heck happened? Where have you been? You look like you've seen a ghost!" And I replied, "Tim, I had a life confession, you won't believe it." He said, "I believe it. Why do you think Our Lady invited you here?" We got to talking and I told him the whole story. I had learned an awful lot through this experience and so I began to think, "*Now* I can be in the presence of the Blessed Mother."

The next day we went right up to pray the Stations at Cross Mountain. Tim and his friend Sean walked up barefoot. I had enough trouble doing it with sneakers on! We prayed and cried and when we reached the top, it was beautiful. I really did not want to leave.

Tim knew the visionary Ivan, and we went to his chapel every day and, within two nights, Ivan invited us to accompany him as he had a private apparition. We went to see visionary Vicka in the village and she prayed over me. Two days later, it was 100 degrees, and we were on Apparition Hill. Usually I would have been at the beach or in the pool in weather like this, and I thought to myself, "What am I doing here, praying between two mountains?" I was trying to follow what was happening. We were going up the rocky hill in the heat to pray the Rosary. We walked up the Joyful Mystery side; there were about 100 people there. Maria Paulic, owner of the Two Hearts Hotel (where we were staying) led a group from Ohio and we decided to join them. As we were going up the hill, I got separated from the group. I saw Tim on the side. I walked around another larger group to get further up the hill. Then I saw a woman sitting on a rock and she had a stack of file cards. I know now that they were prayer intentions. She was older, about seventy, and she looked kind of sickly, so I glanced down and I asked her, "Are you okay?" She stared at me and said, "Give me your hand, young man." So I gave her my hand and pulled her up. She said, "You are going to help me up this hill to visit Our Lady and bring her these prayer intentions." Now, I had recent back problems that had prevented me from playing golf, and it had never entered my mind to help her. But I said to myself, "I just got to help this lady." So this forty-minute journey from the bottom of the hill to the statue of Our Lady turned into a two-and-a-half-hour excursion. I met Tim about three-quarters of the way up the hill as he was helping this woman's friend. The two of us were helping these women up the hill.

When we got there, we were exhausted. I asked Tim, "All well and good, we got them up here, but how the heck are we going to get them down?" I was worried because I figured it would be harder getting them down. Tim replied, "Just pray." I said, "Come on!" He responded, "Just do what I am telling you to do. Trust in the Lord." I said, "Okay."

After hours in the heat assisting these women, we got them down the hill, they thanked us, and we walked away feeling like we had just helped these ladies do something very special.

The next day at the hotel, we went downstairs for breakfast — well, not really breakfast, just bread and water because it was a Friday and that's a fasting day in Medjugorje. The woman I helped up and down the hill was giving testimony about her pilgrimage to forty people over breakfast. It turns out that she had been sick and was talking about meeting this man on Apparition Hill who was her guardian angel helping her take her prayer intentions to Our Lady. I was standing behind her, and she didn't know I was there. I said to myself, "You've got to be kidding me!" I took a few moments to gather myself. Tim and I were going to sit at another table a few feet away, then she stopped talking and she shouted, "There's my guardian angel!" And she introduced me to everybody in her group and I was crying again. Even though my parents had both died young, God had given me the opportunity to be a son again to a woman I didn't even know. God was asking me to serve her, to help her and to test me to see if I was going to listen to His inspiration and obey, or if I was going to walk away. So I said, "Okay. God forgave me in confession, I did this act of service for her, and then I was rewarded because when I came into that room, she was speaking about me." That tied it all in for me, what I had done with a simple "Yes." God can do a lot with a simple "Yes" from us.

Tim recalls that moment too: "I vividly remember looking on as my good friend was overwhelmed with emotion and was sobbing in front of a room full of people. It was as if, in an instant, the walls that Andy had worked his whole life to build were brushed away by the hand of the Lord. As the walls tumbled, so too did Andy's tears. That image will forever be seared into my memory. It is a true testament to the Christ's Divine Mercy."

The third big event on my first trip to Medjugorje happened when I was introduced to the writings of Father Slavko Barbaric about fasting. Neither fasting nor Medjugorje was ever on my radar before. However, in fasting, I had found a practice that assisted me both spiritually and physically on this pilgrimage, so I felt compelled to learn more about it. I wondered, "How come the rest of the church is not practicing it, especially if the

Blessed Mother is recommending it?" I started reading about fasting a few days before we returned home. The best books written were by Father Slavko, and in Medjugorje, the people there told me he held many fasting retreats until his death in November of 2000.

Then, on our last night in Medjugorje, I was sitting on the porch overlooking Apparition Hill at three a.m. I heard a group of Italian women a few feet below, singing the *Ave Maria* while praying the Rosary and I decided to join them. So I sat with them to pray, and then I felt like I was getting some kind of a message from above. "Fasting breads," I heard. Again, I heard in my heart the term, "fasting breads." I asked myself, "What is a 'fasting bread?'"

On the flight home, when Tim and I were returning from our trip, there were many thoughts racing through my head. He begged me to let him sleep, but I kept poking him every time I read something else amazing about fasting. My entire world view had changed, leaving so many burning questions demanding an answer: How would I describe my experience to my family back home? Why am I living at this time in history? What is my purpose in life? What did God create me for? How am I to re-pay God? When can I come back to Medjugorje? The biggest question which remained in my mind was: What on earth is 'fasting bread'? You would think that after thirty-eight years in the bakery industry, I would understand this term!

As I pondered the incredible changes that occurred in me during my miraculous week in Medjugorje, I knew one thing for sure. Although I only realized it then, at age fifty-five, Our Lady's guiding hand had been upon me since my childhood. She was there when my mom asked me to pray a Hail Mary on my walk to Saint Francis De Sales School. Her statue on my path to school was a reminder of her loving protection, even though I was barely aware of it as I passed by. I took my faith for granted as I grew up, involved in the violent life of Charlestown, but she was there, interceding for me. Our Lady was calling me while I worked around the clock to build my business and pursue fame at the racetrack. She continued to wait patiently for me, as I attended Mass sporadically and left early when it interfered with my golf game. Slowly and surely, I recognized her gentle motherly influence in my life, though if you had asked me at that time, I couldn't have told you why I began to attend Mass more regularly. I didn't know why I began a relationship with Fr. Copp, but My Mother did. I now know that Our Lady, Mother Mary, was behind my decision to accept the challenge of teaching C.C.D. to rowdy adolescent boys. Our Lady used Jim Caviezel, who gave her his heart and his acting career, to issue a challenge to me, who never was known to refuse a challenge, to go to an obscure village in Croatia to pray. It was there, at the foot of her statue, the statue which overlooked my childhood that I finally surrendered to her gentle power, saying "Yes" to coming to Medjugorje. Tim Van Damm was there to guide me to Medjugorje to the table where Father Michael Lightner accepted my challenge to leave a feast, and help me go through a life confession. Our Lady had orchestrated it all out of her love for me.

Our Lady has a way of showing us a different path, and she certainly did with me. I am forever grateful for her love, and for the direction she used to bring me back to her Son. The best advice I got to try and to reflect and answer these questions was from Jim Caviezel, who said, "Have patience and trust in God, but most of all, you now can follow the peace in your heart. You are part of Our Lady's Plan."

Chapter Three Bottom Line

Third Gift of the Holy Spirit is Counsel

After I parked in front of the Blessed Mother's statue on Bunker Hill Street, my intuition told me I needed to go to Medjugorje. Our Heavenly Mother Mary is always there for us. I soon learned that she is closer than we think and is urgently begging us to return to her Son. I read the definition of counsel and believe this is all supernatural. She was continuously giving me counsel, but it was not until I surrendered in confession that I was able to stand on my own two feet for the truth.

Ask Our Lady for her counsel in prayer, but especially pray the Rosary to ask her to intercede in your life. Believe me, she will assist you.

I needed to grasp the concept that where Our Lady is, her Spouse, the Holy Spirit, can also be found. For my entire life, I carried animosity for those who offended me. Our Lady showed me how to be patient, forgiving, humble and to love my enemies.

My dream is, as I walk through the door of death, the Blessed Mother is standing there waiting for me. She takes my hand as she says, "Follow me; I am taking you to see my Son."

Counsel, the third gift of the Holy Spirit, is the perfection of the cardinal virtue of prudence. Prudence can be practiced by anyone, but counsel is supernatural. Through this gift of the Holy Spirit, we are able to judge how best to act almost by intuition. Because of the gift of counsel, Christians need not fear to stand up for the truths of the Faith, because the Holy Spirit will guide us in defending those truths.

Source:
http://catholicism.about.com/od/beliefsteachings/p/Counsel.htm

Photographs

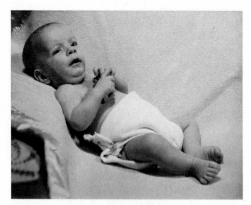

November 1954

My parents, St. Patrick's Day, 1974

January 25, 1975

His 4th win in a row: Irish Lament!

St. Francis de Sales Church, Bunker Hill Street

Statue of Our Lady, Bunker Hill Street

Tim (right) and I (left) in Medjugorje June, 2010

August 2013: Cross Mountain, Medjugorje
It's difficult climbing up, but much joy at the top.

Cross Mountain, Medjugorje

Pilgrims climbing Apparition Hill in Medjugorje to be with Our Lady

Jim Caviezel is a big fan of the 1980 U.S. Olympic Hockey Team

Our family chapel at home

*Mixing fasting bread dough
for the pilgrims in Medjugorje*

*October 2009: Walking my daughter Nicole down the aisle.
That's Jack 'O.C.' (in the light suit)
over my right shoulder, always has an opinion.*

From Children to Business Partners, Jeff, Nicole and I

Barbara and I dancing at Darcie's wedding, 2014
courtesy George Martell, photographer

Chapter 4
Fasting Makes the Impossible Possible

The apartment where my wife and I live in Boston is on the thirteenth floor overlooking Boston Harbor. It was the fall of 2010. I was in my home office, looking out the fifteen-by-fifteen-foot wall of glass windows. The weather outside was a pea soup fog. You couldn't see ten feet in front of you. I was sitting in a chair in the reading section of the room, and thinking about the topic of fasting which kept coming up while we were in Medjugorje.

I was considering the question, "What is fasting?" That's a good question, because it's really not often taught or practiced today. Our Lady is calling us to fast. In a 1984 apparition, she said, "Fast strictly on Wednesday and Friday." These two days signify the Betrayal, the Passion and Death of Jesus. We are all called to conversion through prayer and fasting as a team. I think it's hard to focus on prayer with a full stomach. In Pope Benedict's 2009 Lenten message, he defines fasting as, "A great help to avoid sin and all that leads to it." Boy that really describes me! Whenever I got into trouble, it typically first started with a great dinner or excessive drinking, maybe a prideful cigar, and then the trouble sprang up. Afterward, I usually asked myself, "How did I get here?" So I really understand what the Holy Father is saying.

Today we hear the term abstinence used interchangeably with fasting. I learned quickly there is a big difference. Abstinence is giving up a specific food for a period of time and a term often used in Lent. When Lent comes around, the most common question is, "What are you giving up?" The typical answer goes, "For Lent I am giving up chocolate." Big deal! Jesus was betrayed, scourged, crucified and died for our sins, and we're giving up chocolate? Have you ever seen the scourging scene in *The Passion of Christ*?

Look, I am not trying to be critical here. However, the point is that the world around us is not willing to change, so we need to look to change individually, one by one. Fasting is the tool to change your outlook most effectively. Fasting is a lot more serious than abstinence; it's like going from high school baseball to Fenway Park. It really is the major league of spirituality. Before every significant event in biblical history, Christ and His disciples fasted. It was *that* important. Jesus showed us by teaching the apostles to fast in order to cast out demons, and proved that nothing is impossible through prayer and fasting. In Our Lady's fasting messages at Medjugorje, she is calling us to fast only on bread and water, for 24 hours each Wednesday and Friday. Now *that* is a serious commitment.

My definition of fasting is a total emptying of ourselves of food and drink. No coffee, butter, jam, jelly, just plain bread and water. By the way, it's bread for a few great reasons. First, Jesus said, *"I am the Bread of life, whoever comes to me will never hunger, and whoever believes in me will never thirst."* (*John 6:35*) The words hunger and thirst make it clear to me that Jesus is referring to bread and water. The second and most important reason to use bread in fasting is that it relates to the Holy Eucharist. I was educated in the importance of attending daily Mass and craving Jesus in the Eucharist. It always helped when I attended Mass on fasting days.

As long as we are talking about Christ in the Eucharist, it must be said that we need to reinstate the true Eucharistic fast. No coffee, soda, or food one hour before communion, just plain water. The use of water is the component for our cleansing and purification. For centuries, this form of fasting has been the perfect remedy to prepare us to receive Holy Communion.

Father Slavko has written two great books on fasting, and in them, he says, "When a man lives on earthly bread alone, he discovers the importance of the Eucharistic bread, and his eyes are open to the fullness of life." He also said, "Practically speaking, fasting goes beyond the realm of food into our actions and thoughts." I can absolutely agree that my actions — and especially my thoughts — have been much holier with fasting.

Father Slavko was assigned to the Medjugorje parish of Saint James in 1983, a few years after the apparitions started. He had a doctorate in religious pedagogy and was a psychotherapist. So it was his responsibility to prove the apparitions false. However, he had a very open approach to the messages, and soon came to believe in their authenticity and eventually became the ambassador to pilgrims from the entire world. He began assisting the visionaries and it was not long before nothing could separate him from promoting Our Lady's messages. He *was* Medjugorje. His fasting retreats were legendary; bread and water only for a week. To him, fasting was as important as prayer and they were a team that could not be separated. The saints were well aware of the benefits of fasting. St Peter Chrysologus said, *"Fasting is the soul of prayer; mercy is the lifeblood of fasting. Let no one try to separate them, they cannot be separated."*

Father Slavko is not saying that prayer is not powerful, but rather, the extraordinary power of prayer combined with fasting cannot be denied. In fact, Our Lady says "Prayer and fasting are so powerful they can stop wars." Later in this book, we will see a modern day example of what she is talking about. She also says, "Other than the Eucharist, the most powerful weapon against Satan is prayer and fasting." In our world today, we are having a tough time defeating evil. I think it's time we start listening to her. Father Slavko in his book *Fast with The Heart* says, "Without prayer and fasting, God's plan cannot be realized, so our cooperation is very, very, important." Remember Jesus said in Matthew's Gospel, *"But when you fast, anoint your hair and wash your face..." (Matt 6:17)* This means He expected us to do it. Jesus did not say to consider fasting.

I had never fasted before in my life, but while I was in Medjugorje it really struck me how much energy I had while fasting. We climbed Apparition Hill and Cross Mountain on fast days. I was amazed by the increased alertness I had throughout the day. My friends and I adhered to the Wednesday and Friday twenty-four-hour bread and water fast. When we fasted, we made a pact, encouraging and supporting each other. We all understood if the hunger pangs came, that it was a good thing and it was time to pray. I was thinking about trying to live the rest of my life just as we did during the pilgrimage in Medjugorje. During my time there, I was asking myself, "Could I grow to have a deeper, more meaningful prayer life?" I had started to go to daily Mass, do daily Scripture reading. Going to confession was now a regular occurrence, and my Rosary was always with me in my pocket. But I learned that I needed to fast as well.

Be careful when you decide to fast. The road will always start with temptation. Just like Jesus, preparing for his ministry in the desert by fasting forty days and nights, most spiritual journeys begin with the temptation to not start in the first place. Jesus has shown us by fasting we can fight through the evil temptations. My thoughts were, "Fasting on a regular basis? I don't think so: I am married to an Italian who can cook." Can you see the pull? The similarity is that most temptation not to fast starts in the gut.

I really loved getting away and drinking a pint of beer with my buddies. This had been a big part of my life. Remember, though, that my thoughts and my heart were now showing me how important it is to follow Our Lady's call to fast. Once I got home, the big challenge would be: Could I be disciplined enough?

I have always been one to go the extreme in almost everything. I began to see fasting as a tool to help me defeat the temptations that kept entering my thoughts. Could fasting be the discipline to help me be self-controlled and help support my new beginning? Would fasting twice a week be a solution to control the vices that were destroying my life? My attendance at daily Mass had already shocked my friends and family. I wasn't sure they could take any more changes in me!

It was only a few months into my conversion, but I noticed that with fasting, my prayer life was dramatically different. I had recently learned that the Greek word for repentance, *metanoia*, means a transforming of the mind. Fasting was doing its job, transforming my mind and, through repentance and frequent confession, was cleansing my soul. The more I became committed to fasting, the better my interior life felt.

In fact, this reminds me of a story I was told by Sister Emmanuel (who you will read about in a later chapter). There was a young man who had an infection in his leg. He tried to clean it and took some medicine, but nothing seemed to work. The infection started to spread rapidly and he was rushed to the doctor. The doctor took one look at it, then referred the boy to the specialist. The specialist took a sample of the infection and sent it to the lab. The doctor came back to the boy with good news. He said, "We have found the cure for your infection, but it's a twofold cure, and I am sure that the remedy will bring your leg back to 100% good health." He emphasized that the two aspects of the cure must be used together for his infection to be cured. This is how prayer and fasting work as a team. They must be used together to restore our lives.

I don't know about you, but I am very concerned about the world today, especially the sinful nature of the United States, which seems to be deteriorating rapidly. The Great Physician, Our Lord Himself, has assured us that prayer and fasting will bring results, and create change even in the most critical situations.

I can tell you that prayer and fasting work. How do I know that? Well, sometimes you're a skeptic until you experience it yourself, and yes, that was me. I had to learn firsthand, the hard way, to believe they worked exceptionally well as a team. The truth is that my total conversion would not be possible without the discipline of fasting.

Sin had a deep hold on me and something had to give. What type of sin, you might ask? Well here goes. I really never said that I wanted to stop drinking, swearing and lying, but when I fasted, it caused a renewal of my soul. Prayer and fasting helped me to overcome all the impure thoughts, the vulgar mouth with which I swore 1500 times a day, the disrespect and pre-judging of all mankind, the drinking excessively, the prideful talk and the lying to everyone about who I was. Gradually it all was taken away, not by me, but by an Almighty and Merciful God who had plans for me to work on His team. I cannot explain it, but it all worked out as long as I said "Yes" to fasting. He took care of everything else.

Fasting taught me great discipline with other areas of my life. When I fast, I feel an incredible freedom. When I have the courage to surrender and place all my concerns in God's hands, for Him to deal with my intentions, I have an overwhelming sense of elation and joy. It is like a strong adrenaline rush in which fasting is no longer an obligation for me, but fills me with a God-centered love, a love of knowing that I participate in a practice that Jesus Himself did, His Mother Mary did, and the Apostles and saints did. I now have a feeling of anticipation that I cannot wait for the next fast day!

Fasting is the window to an ongoing process of spiritual change. In the bakery world, yeast makes everything grow. Fasting is the yeast of conversion. It gradually takes over us, but we remain ourselves, and we are made into a better version of ourselves, one that the Holy Spirit permeates so that in God's plan we become a light in the dark world to reach out to others. I am convinced that we can have a transformed Church with fasting as a major practice.

Our new Saint Pope John Paul II said this about fasting in his *1994 Letter to Families*, "Jesus has shown us by His own example that prayer and fasting are the first and most effective weapon against the forces of evil."

Let me explain how once you begin fasting, you start feeling so good. Food has a tremendous hold on us. It's very hard to get away from the foods you desire. The food industry has laced all our foods with many chemicals to make us crave more, more and more. This craving hurts our spiritual growth by placing the focus on food and not on God. From a health perspective, fasting cleanses our body from these toxins and makes us feel so much healthier. The physical, medical and long-term effects of fasting have been and continue to be studied by doctors and scientists throughout the world. According to Dr. Michael Mosley, who has written extensively on fasting, especially two days a week, "Scientists are only just beginning to discover and prove how powerful a tool it can be." In 2011, Fox News featured a segment on fasting, with Dr. Rosenfeld who said that, "Cultures which fast on a regular basis have fewer health risks than other people." So fasting can help you both physically and spiritually.

One of the greatest advantages of fasting is that it increases one's awareness to listen to the direction of the Holy Spirit. I can remember after I returned from Medjugorje, I went to my golf club in South Carolina. I loved it there because it was not only a place to play golf, but it was also a center of fellowship. One afternoon, after thirty-six holes of golf, we were sitting on the porch with about twenty guys telling stories and having a few cold pints. My friend Pete from Chicago stepped up in front of everybody and said, "Andy, I played golf with you the last two days, and now we have been here on the porch for over an hour, and I have not heard you say f*&*# once. What is going on in your life?" Well, Pete was referring to my reputation of a complete trash mouth in conversation; I could swear with the best of them. So now he was calling me out in front of twenty guys who wanted to know the answer to his question.

Remember I mentioned earlier about increased awareness? Well, right after the question from Pete, I sensed God in my heart saying, "Are you going to tell them the truth about Me in your life or you going to just brush Me under the rug?" Both God and Pete were putting me on the spot, and they wanted answers! I told them the truth. I had been fasting, praying the Rosary, attending Adoration, doing Scripture reading and going to frequent confession. In the mornings, I had been sneaking across the street to Saint Peter's Church for daily Mass. They all had witnessed a dramatic change in me, but only Pete was willing to challenge me to tell them. A funny thing happened the next morning before breakfast. I went across the street at 6:15 a.m. to attend daily Mass and pray a Rosary. Just before Mass began, I turned around and there were four golf buddies sitting a few rows behind me! God works in funny ways!

Our Lady is the key to everything. Did you ever mail a letter, and it takes a long time to get there, and you wonder how come it's taking so long? Here is what I know about Our Lady and her mission to bring us all back to her Son Jesus. If you want the absolute, positively overnight to Jesus Himself, you go through Our Lady. She is the FedEx, the absolute best way to her Son. It's guaranteed overnight, no ifs, ands or buts about it! Each day, my love for Our Lady grows deeper and deeper.

So, as I sat in my chair that autumn day, staring out the window into the fog, I sensed it was time to pray a Rosary. As I prayed, I could not get my mind off fasting. So after the Rosary, I picked up Father Slavko Barbaric's first book on fasting. I could not shake this reference to fasting in my mind, so I decided to ask Our Lady in my heart, "Do you want me to do something here? What is this about fasting?" As soon as I asked the question, a beam of light came out of the clouds and hit me on the side of the cheek. I had my head in the book, but I felt the warmth of the light on my face, so I looked up and that beam of light was there for fifteen seconds. Then it was gone. I was left wondering what that meant. I realize, as I try to walk this path, that things do not happen on my terms, but on God's terms, and clarification usually comes one step at a time.

Chapter Four Bottom Line

Fourth Gift of the Holy Spirit is Fortitude

God has given us every tool we need to survive here on this earthly pilgrimage. The devil is very strong; evil is winning in our world. We are losing the battle for life, for family, for religious freedom. The persecutions are strong. How do we stand and fight the powers of darkness?

We find our example in the lives of the saints who built the Church through prayer and fasting. There is hope with fasting, but it takes fortitude. Try it like I did and you will see the results as your life starts to change. This change and conversion are available to those willing to sacrifice the things of the world which get in the way of spiritual progress. For me, there was no quicker, more consistent practice to bring me closer to God than fasting combined with prayer.

Try it. You have nothing to lose and everything to gain!

While counsel is the perfection of a cardinal virtue, fortitude is both a gift of the Holy Spirit and a cardinal virtue. Fortitude is ranked as the fourth gift of the Holy Spirit because it gives us the strength to follow through on the actions suggested by the gift of counsel. While fortitude is sometimes called courage, it goes beyond what we normally think of as courage. Fortitude is the virtue of the martyrs that allows them to suffer death rather than to renounce the Christian Faith.

Source:
http://catholicism.about.com/od/beliefsteachings/p/Fortitude.htm

Chapter 5

Six Life-Changing Habits That Work For Me

Each day, every one of us has the decision to accept or reject the love of God which heals and renews our souls. His major way of providing this love is His giving of Himself to us through the sacraments. In grammar school, I was taught by the nuns that the sacraments are required. Today I look at them as gifts. I learned the hard way that the sacraments are the tools we need to keep us on the right path to improvement. As I explained in Chapter Two, I did not pay much attention to the Holy Spirit and His direction. For a long time, I took the spiritual tools and minimized them, making up my own rules, choosing rather to focus on maximizing success in the material things. I was driven to achieve in this world. There is no doubt now that my goals are different.

I talk pretty regularly about the battle between good and evil. The real battle is between the body and the soul. When the evil one has an influence on our body, we usually take the easiest path. What I mean by easiest path is that when I have the opportunity to eat healthy, I usually take the easiest path and select the junk food that I crave. My flesh often wins over my soul. The soul must control the body, not the body control the soul. Jesus warned against this. If we allow this to happen, the result is that the soul will be lost.

My friend, Father Michael Nolan, has taught me that the destination of the soul is more important than that of the body. I take full responsibility for what I did, but now in order to remain on God's team, I need the sacraments. They give me strength to battle the evil temptations each day. In this chapter, I hope to outline for you the tools that I use, and how to maintain and persevere on the path towards gaining virtues that will lead to eternal life in Heaven with Our Lord.

If I took anything from Jim Caviezel's talk at the Boston Catholic Men's Conference, it's this: God is far more powerful than evil and, in the end, no matter what difficulties you experience in this earthly life, Christ wins. So what side you're on will totally depend upon you!

Confession

Let us first address the Sacrament of Confession. In my lifetime, I had been to confession numerous times, but it never really affected me like my life confession in Medjugorje. This little village between the hills in Bosnia is often nicknamed "The Confessional of the World." That is because they have over sixty confessionals in all different languages. Yes, sixty...and the lines are longer than at Disney World, so go figure! If you ask a priest who has been on pilgrimage there, he will tell you that he was deeply impacted by hearing the confessions in Medjugorje. I chose confession first because for me it is the beginning sacrament. Most all conversions start with confession.

In Father Slavko's book *Give Me Your Wounded Heart*, he says this about the greatest sin and confession: "Where love is missing, the doors are wide open to evil. All wars, family and personal conflicts, all injustices stem from and are consequences of the lack of love. The absence of love is our greatest sin." I love this book because it addresses the sacrament from the perspective of our hearts. In my life confession, I received the love, mercy and forgiveness of Our Lord so I, in turn, could love others unconditionally, regardless of the result. I say regardless of the result because I have found that even the closest people to you, your family and friends, are going to hurt you. It was a great lesson for me to learn to forgive and not hold a grudge. To be able to love unconditionally, I first needed to understand what Jesus did for me in the Sacrament of Reconciliation.

During our pilgrimage, there were many first-time experiences in Medjugorje. Looking back, I can admit that this was the first time in my life I sincerely felt truly sorry for offending God. In the past, I was definitely able to lie to my wife and those who loved me. But in confession, it was unveiling the real truth that God the Father in heaven already knew about me and my actions, yet He loved me as a sinner. I just had to be accountable and tell the truth.

There is no fooling God. All actions, big or small, have consequences. Small sins can lead to bigger sins, if you let them. As I cried my heart out in this sacrament, I felt my true sorrow lead to an overwhelming sense of repentance that brought me to conversion. The feeling was so powerful that it created a genuine healing in my heart. God has so much to give us but, in confession, you receive an immense source of grace joined with unlimited loving gifts from above.

For most of us, going to confession to a priest can be uncomfortable or embarrassing. We are revealing all our weaknesses, bad habits and immorality to another person. Please understand, this is not just another person; it's a priest designated by God the Father to administer the sacraments. Some of us decide not to go just because we do not like it. I used to treat it like going to the dentist. I hated it. As a teenager, I did everything I could to get out of it.

Now I go to confession weekly, and if I walk by a confessional and the door is open, I go in because it's available, even if it's only been a few days.

Here is a somewhat funny story about going to confession the next day. On Saturday afternoon, I was in a meeting with my spiritual director and had just gone to confession. Later, I returned home, put on the TV, and suddenly my mind was fighting these impure thoughts, created by my choice of viewing. So the next day before Sunday Mass, I walked by, and the door to the confessional was open. I felt this compelling invitation, especially for me to confess my sins. I walked into the confessional and began, "Bless me, Father, for I have sinned. It's been one day since my last confession." It turns out the priest administering the sacrament was my spiritual director who I met with yesterday, so he responded, "Welcome back, my brother. What brings you here after one day?" We both laughed. Great confessors will always make you feel comfortable.

The priest confessor is very important. You can search for months trying to find the right priest. I like someone who is going to give it to me straight. A good confessor will be able to identify the symptoms of the sins you're committing, and give you suggestions on how to fix these actions. He will also encourage you or caution you about the direction you are taking. His penance will directly correlate with your sins. Remember that penance is not punishment. It comes with the joy of prayer as we restore our relationship with Christ. When I go to confession, I have complete trust in the priest, and doing so allows me to feel a real meeting between heaven and earth.

God is truly present in this sacrament. Just go and try it for yourself. Remember the old Nike brand commercial, "Just Do It." Well, if you 'just do it,' the graces are many. Like anything else, it will be a better result if you prepare. Do an examination of conscience to consider your sins. You can find this on the Internet under, "Catholic Examination of

Conscience for Adults." I usually make a list of my sins on a scrap piece of paper before going in. Just do not forget to destroy the list after the sacrament.

Most importantly, tell *all* your sins. Do not hold any back. I never realized when I gave a partial account of my sins, that it turned out not to be a valid confession. God knows my every thought and my every move, and I owe it to Him to tell Him I am truly sorry.

Let us talk about sin here. Our time we spend here, along with actions, will determine our destination in eternity. It's no joke. One thing I quickly learned about sin is that I had to resolve to avoid the company and the places that might tempt me to sin. My car had to get used to traveling to my favorite chapel and not to my favorite tavern where I could get into some real trouble if I went in. For me, this was a difficult change.

The first type of sin is mortal, and it's more dangerous. If it is not redeemed by repentance and God's forgiveness, it causes exclusion from Christ's Kingdom and results in eternal death in hell. (*Catechism #1861*) Indeed, hell is real. The math is simple. Mortal sin equals hell if there is no sacrament of confession or forgiveness in the form of God's graces. This type of sin destroys our relationship with a loving God. So do I really want to take that risk?

For a sin to be *mortal*, three conditions must together be met: "Mortal sin is sin whose object is grave matter and which is also committed with full knowledge and deliberate consent." This is from the *Catechism of Catholic Church*, and the key here is full knowledge and with deliberate consent. What does that mean? It means that when you convince yourself, "It's not that bad," or "It's okay to do it, most of the time," it's not. You have just had a conversation with yourself and made up your own rules. I used to do it all the

95

time. You have given yourself permission to sin. This was a serious problem for me, generated by my large sin of pride.

If you're serious about sorting this all out, there is a great web reference at www.saintaquinas.com/mortalsin that explains it very clearly. They point out that all of the Ten Commandments are being compromised each day by all men and women through our 'made-up' understanding mortal sin. Here is one example in my case. The fifth commandment is "Thou shalt not kill." The literal sense is to murder or kill. For me I damaged my body and soul through the abuse of alcohol, which lead to gluttony, then it brought on anger, along with hatred and revenge. Now count that up: one commandment, five mortal sins. All these are not accidents since they were chosen freely. This is why God gave us the Sacrament of Confession. We all need a reset button, and consistent confession can change all that.

Venial sin is the other type of sin. It is a lot less serious but can impede our spiritual progress and lead to serious sin. For me, most bad habits reinforce and strengthen vices which lead to mortal sin. In society today, we have diluted the cause and effect of sin. I assure you that God knows each and every sin, and we will have to account for them on Judgment Day. Do you ever watch TV golf and look a few minutes later to see your favorite player fall off the leader board? Well, those bogey and double bogeys (i.e. venial sins) will keep you off the leader board and away from God's grace. This is what I am trying to say here.

A simple white lie with the help of the devil can lead to a serious sin and terrible heartbreak. I know because I have been there. I deeply hurt those who love me, and then sadly asked myself what happened to me, how did I get here?

To repeat, the big difference here is mortal sin leads to the breaking of our relationship with God, and venial sins are less serious sins that can lead to mortal sin, if we're not careful. The only way to restore this is through confession. Every confession is a new beginning on life.

In Scott Hahn's book *Lord Have Mercy,* he says the Sacrament of Penance is made up of two equally essential elements. There's our work of a repentant sinner, and then there's God's work through the action of the Holy Spirit. I agree that the Holy Spirit is the principal agent of confession.

Let me wrap up confession with a quote from Father Slavko's book *Give Me Your Wounded Heart:* "The Sacrament of Confession surpasses any other human meeting, because in confession the penitent meets with God." For me, I can vouch for this: the relationship is vertical: me, the priest and God.

Holy Mass and the Eucharist

I was recently giving a talk at Northeastern University Catholic Center on Business Ethics and how it relates to Catholic Social Doctrine. I had baked many samples of variety breads for the students to taste. During the Q & A section, a student asked me the following: "Mr. LaVallee, we have tasted Focaccia, Ciabatta, Baguettes, a Butter Brioche, and even Pretzel Bread. Which bread in your career is your favorite?"

I answered the question this way: "All these breads are great breads for different purposes when it comes to your specific taste or menu usage, but none of these will get you to eternal life. My favorite bread is the Bread of Life, the Holy Eucharist."

Why is it called the Bread of Life? I know that what I am going to say may not be popular here, but here is the truth. Real life occurs at the time of death. Death is going to happen for all of us; it's a fact. No more suffering, conflicts, family wars, sickness, temptations from evil; it all goes away, and we will either live with God Our Father in Paradise or live forever in hell without Him. What struck me in my conversion is that I needed to stop living for today, but for tomorrow. I was also big on living *my* way, and now it was central to focus on the afterlife and rebuild my relationship with God. It was plain to understand that I will never be able to live this life properly until I understand what happens after death. The Holy Eucharist is the new life. Understanding what happens after death can only be explained in Scripture, and Our Lord's promise that He would save a place for us: *"In my Father's house there are many dwelling places. If there were not, would I have told you that I am going to prepare a place for you? And if I go and prepare a place for you, I will come back again and take you to myself, so that where I am you also may be." (John 14:2-3)* After reading that, I only ask, "What is the occupancy rate going to be?"

I believe the best way to prepare for the after life is to unite ourselves to Him through gifts of the Eucharist. These gifts come in two forms, first, the Body of Christ, and second, the Blood of Christ. During the Holy Mass, the holy gifts are consecrated and become the authentic Body and Blood of our Savior, Jesus Christ. By partaking in the Mass and receiving Our Lord, we are given the hope, love and life to live in unity with Christ for eternity. For me, it's that simple. I desperately want to go to eternal life with Christ, so I go to daily Mass and receive Him, to prepare, and cleanse me for the judgment day to come. This is also one of the best ways for Jesus and me to get to know each other and to truly create a loving relationship.

I need to prepare for the real encounter with Jesus at

Mass. I do this by honoring the Eucharistic fast. It means nothing consumed or eaten one hour before Mass. We are allowed plain water and nothing else: no coffee, juice or soda. I need to make room for Him each day in my life. I need the Holy Eucharist to survive in my world today. (Medications for the sick and elderly are allowed and may, if necessary, be consumed during the Eucharistic fast.)

In the past I put no emphasis on attending Mass and, if I attended, I arrived minutes beforehand with no preparation. Today I attend Mass every day, and I need to move towards better preparation for this sacred encounter. I tell myself that I should arrive half an hour early, pray the Rosary, and then call on the Holy Spirit in prayer to help me stay focused on the Sacrifice and Gift of the Mass. Today I look at the Mass as the highest living value you can get in the world today. It's a value that is measured by the depth of our love for Him and His unconditional love for us. If I place myself at the Last Supper, Jesus commanded us to partake in the Eucharist by saying, *"Do this in remembrance of Me."* You can never go wrong following His commands.

It's time for a story in this regard. During the summer, at Saint Clement's Eucharistic Shrine, the seminarians end class and return home. This creates a major need for Eucharistic ministers at the altar. I was briefly almost half-asked to do this, but when the call never came, I was emotionally drained and disappointed. With my conversion and daily Mass participation, I was thinking God might ask me to do this. I got my hopes up and considered it a great honor. Weeks went by. Then on a Saturday morning, I got a call to come in before Mass for training. When I met the soon-to-be-priest Brother John at the door for training, I wept openly in front of everyone when he asked me to be a Eucharistic minister. No one knew what was going on in my mind.

For years I lived in this world that taught me that my actions made me unworthy, that I was an imposter, with impurity, spoke lies, and sinfulness that prevented me from approaching God. I pushed away instead of trying to seek Him. Now it was possible that He was considering me to assist in distributing His precious Body and Blood. What struck me here was that it is only important how God sees you, and not how the world sees you, or how you see yourself. So when Brother John asked me to be a Eucharistic minister, I could not hold back my emotions, and it was clear for me to understand that, by this gift, God certainly saw me differently than I saw myself, and for me this was coming directly from God above.

One thing about the Gift of the Holy Eucharist I realize as I gaze into the chalice or choose the next Host to distribute: it does not matter what the shape or how broken the Sacred Host is. Every piece and every particle is the true presence of God in the Eucharist. God is not giving of Himself in a material way, but in a sacramental way. He is unlimited.

To speak of the Holy Eucharist and the great gift of Mass, it takes more than a layman, and certainly more than a bread man. It takes one of my heroes, Cardinal Raymond Burke, who consecrates these divine gifts to us each day. In the book, *The Eucharistic Miracles of the World,* he sums it all up in his foreword for this book. He says, "The Holy Eucharist is the source at which Christ's life is nourished within us with the incomparable food which is His Body, Blood, and Divinity. The Holy Eucharist is the highest expression of our life in Christ, for it unites us sacramentally to Christ in the sacrifice of the Cross, which is made always new in the celebration of Holy Mass."

Divine Mercy Devotion

Plain and simple, if I am going to trust in God, I need to pray the Divine Mercy Chaplet and understand the concept of Divine Mercy. Our Lord says, "Mankind will not have peace until it turns with trust to God's Mercy." (*Divine Mercy in My Soul*, 300) I have found in my own life of prayer that binding myself to the prayer, "Jesus I Trust in You," gives me comfort and calm knowing that there is no need for fear if I am really fully trusting in Him — and I emphasize fully!

Saint Maria Faustina Kowalska is known to the world as the "Apostle of the Divine Mercy." Through the leadership of then Archbishop Karol Wojtyla in the 1960's, the information was gathered on her diary entitled, *Divine Mercy in my Soul*, and the messages concerning the Divine Mercy of Our Lord. Jesus had appeared to her for a very important mission. Sister Maria Faustina was to bring the message of Divine Mercy to the World. The connection and relationship between Pope John Paul II and Sister Faustina is really astonishing. It's another real fact that shows how God works in our life.

It was Karol Wojtyla, as Archbishop of Krakow, Poland who, after Saint Faustina's death, was the first to consider bringing Saint Faustina's name before the Congregation of Saints for consideration as worthy of being put forward for beatification.

On Divine Mercy Sunday, April 30, 2000, a week after Easter Sunday, the now Pope John Paul II canonized Sister Faustina Kowalska, a saint. In doing so, he also approved the Divine Mercy message and devotion by declaring the Second Sunday of Easter as "Divine Mercy Sunday" for the universal Church. In one of the most extraordinary homilies of his pontificate, Pope John Paul II repeated three times that Saint Faustina is "God's gift to our time."

The heavenly connection is that Pope John Paul II died on Divine Mercy Sunday, 2005. Then, on Divine Mercy Sunday 2014, he was canonized a saint on the same day fourteen years prior that he canonized Sister Faustina.

Divine Mercy Sunday is the day when all God's mercy, graces and gifts flood our world. One of the best things for me about this sacred Sunday is the introduction of the opportunity to receive or give a plenary indulgence. This Divine Mercy indulgence grants a full pardon for all sins committed — yes, *all* sins. For me, I look at this gift as something only God the Father can provide.

This reminds me of growing up and one time my friend and I broke a window playing stick ball. I knew we were in big trouble. To minimize the penalty, I went to my father and told him the truth that we did it. He responded that "It took guts to come over to me and tell the truth, but because you did, I will pay to have the window fixed and please do not do that again." My earthy father was acting as a Heavenly Father does in a plenary indulgence. He paid for the window, forgave the debt of my sin, and cleared the slate, just "try not to do it again." That is the miracle gift of a plenary indulgence. Another example would be that you're baptized, a few seconds later you die and then you get the express to heaven. This is the real appreciation of how much God loves us and wants us to spend eternity with Him.

Here is the coolest thing. You can transfer this indulgence to another person, not living but who has died. I do not know about you, but I have many family members and friends who would love this gift. I do not want to presume God's mercy but it's God's word, a guarantee to transfer the indulgence to someone you love who has passed away, and as long as you meet the conditions of the indulgence, they are in heaven. I like to transfer this gift because first off, it will be a surprise coming from me, and second, I get the prayer I really need of someone who is there with Jesus Christ, the Blessed Virgin Mary and all the angels and saints in heaven.

Yes, I know the small print, "as long as you meet all the conditions." What does that mean? I knew this was too good to be true. These conditions must be brutal. This is exactly what I thought when I first heard of this Divine Gift. It all depends on how you look at it.

The two simple conditions are these. (1) You must be in the state of grace, which means a Sacramental Confession is essential to start. (2) Attend Mass and receive the Holy Eucharist. There are no other gifts like this on the face of the Earth. It ties us directly to the souls in purgatory. There are three times I like to gift the indulgence: Divine Mercy Sunday, the week of All Saints and All Souls in November, and during a pilgrimage to a Holy Site. I recommend that you consult your priest for other times that might qualify.

When doing this, almost always do it on the same day, at the same time, around Holy Mass. So before Mass I go to Confession, then at Mass I receive the Holy Eucharist. After Mass I pray a Rosary for the Pope, then a prayer of thanksgiving to Our Lord, and then hand the indulgence off to the one I love. The reason I do this on the same day around Mass is because if I leave open time between the sacraments, I am opening myself to sin and then everything is invalid. This devotion takes a level of higher focus, whether you're doing this for yourself or a loved one. Sometimes I am guilty of treating this as a transaction. It's not. It's a promise from God. It's a covenant. While at Confession, during Mass and praying for the Holy Father, it's important to keep the focus on the love, mercy and forgiveness of God the Father for His children.

Every day in the three o'clock hour, we gather and pray

the Divine Mercy chaplet. The three o'clock hour is connected directly to Jesus' Passion and the crucifixion. This Chaplet came about as Our Lord Jesus Himself dictated it to Saint Faustina. The prayer is an offering to God the Father for our sins and those of the whole world. At three p.m., it's a great break from whatever you're doing to refocus on the Passion of Christ. If you can pray this prayer in Adoration, then get ready for a mountain of graces coming your way.

Why is all this important? It is written in Sister Faustina's Diary (1541); Jesus Himself said, "It pleases Me to grant everything they ask of Me by saying the chaplet."

As long as we are talking about graces, it's important to realize that for us to maximize our grace quota, you must look at God's desires before your own. One of my most favorite sections in the Diary is Section 1385: "November 19. After Communion today, Jesus told me how much He desires to come to human hearts. 'I desire to unite Myself with human souls...when I come to a heart in Holy Communion, My great delight is to unite Myself with souls. My hands are full of all kinds of graces which I want to give to the soul. But souls do not even pay any attention to Me; they leave Me to Myself and busy themselves with other things. Oh, how sad I am that souls do not recognize Love! They treat Me as a dead object.'"

For many Catholics, when Holy Mass is over, we are off to have coffee and donuts along with errands planned for the day. Or our minds are racing a mile a minute, and there is our friend Joe we must see. Oh well, it's okay. We just got the checkmark for Mass and Communion. We are always thinking of other things, and most anything can distract us during and after Mass. I am the worst at this.

Jesus is begging us to take a minute to close our eyes

and truly meet with Him after we receive Him in The Holy Eucharist. He comes to us in this small piece of bread and unites Himself with us to give His treasures reserved only for us. This, Brother and Sister, is "The Real Purpose of Bread," to unite ourselves with Jesus, to do His will, and to gain entry into Eternity.

One last thought on how deeply I trust in the Divine Mercy. Make no mistake about it. The Blessed Virgin Mary remains beside her Son, the spiritual leader, at the helm of Our Church today. She consistently points everything to her Son, so it is essential to believe that the message of Divine Mercy is at the center of her plan for the world today.

Eucharistic Adoration

Our mind and body get a huge dose of the world through a variety of images daily on TV, internet, billboards, and media. We just do not seem to have time for anybody or anything; we are all so busy. A priest friend once taught me the acronym for busy: Being Under Satan's Yoke. You get the point. For me, Adoration creates a place of peace and quiet where I can meet with, and be with God. Saint Clement's in Boston on Boylston Street, just a few blocks from Fenway Park, has twenty-four hour Adoration. Every day there are thousands of people who walk by and have no idea that God is inside waiting them to take just a minute out of their day and say hello.

If you're like me and did not know what Adoration was up until a few years ago, let me define it in lay terms. The Blessed Sacrament, a large consecrated Eucharist, is placed in a gold stand called a monstrance and put on the altar for us to worship and adore. Yes, the consecration makes it the true presence of God right there in front of you. Some churches do it hourly and others do it perpetually or round-the-clock. The silence and respect for the presence of Jesus allows us to be like a magnet just absorbing His love for each of us. It's like being at the beach on a sunny day, and when the day is over, you take a shower and realize you got burnt by the sun. Well, in Adoration we are gently transformed by a stronger light, the love, the graces and gifts of Jesus Himself. It's an inward transformation that provides a new light in a dark world.

How do we spend our time in Adoration in front of God? I do it in a number of ways. No one way is right or wrong. It's just how you feel and where the Holy Spirit is leading you. First of all, pray the Rosary. In Adoration, time slows down, and you realize at that moment of prayer there is nothing more important than this Hail Mary right now. In silence you can really focus on placing yourself in each mystery of the Rosary as you pray each decade. I particularly like to do this and feel like you're actually there in each scene.

Here is an illustration. The third mystery of the Glorious Mysteries is the Coming of the Holy Spirit to Mary and the Apostles. By now, I know you think I am nuts, but I can honestly say in Adoration I visualize the Blessed Mother inviting me to the upper room to be with her and the Apostles as the Holy Spirit arrives at Pentecost. This prospect in Adoration is as clean and crisp as the smell of freshly cut grass on the golf course.

For me, one of the most powerful prayers for discernment is the practice of Ignatian Discernment. In life we have many options, both pro and con, on how we can make choices, but the spiritual exercises eliminate all the clutter around a decision and bring clarity to the will of God. This practice provides me with the best overall aid to determine the best path to take. I learned this practice from the Oblate priests who taught me that all important decisions can be made by how I listen to my heart, where God communicates most. You measure this by the emotion and depth of God's love. When it's clear what God wants, it's so powerful that I am often moved to tears in this area.

Father Tim Gallagher of the Oblates of the Virgin Mary wrote many books and is considered an expert on Ignatian spirituality. I highly recommend his books and retreats. Start with the book *The Discernment of Spirits: an Ignatian Guide for Everyday Living*. He talks of the rules of discernment as being able to understand the movement which causes the souls to do good and reject evil. In doing so, some are moved to watershed moments in their lives that lead to dedicating their lives to the service of Jesus the King.

Here is what I mean. One time in Adoration, I was practicing Ignatian discernment, and I had asked a very important question of God. I felt deeply moved by God as He spoke to my heart and said *"Be an obedient servant and do not withhold anything from me. If you obey My voice, I will bless you and future generations to come because of your love for Me."* I know this does seem imaginary, but you need to be present to see the movement and how much emotion and love are present, and then you can choose for yourself.

Let me tell you about a most powerful experience. A few weeks before my Adoration hour, I had a dream in which I met the Blessed Mother at the door of death, and she said "Andrew, give me your hand; I will lead you to my Son."

My Adoration hour is twelve a.m. on Sunday morning. I love dedicating the first hour of the week to God. One time it was the middle of the night and I was asking God about possibly working full-time in the fasting ministry. My big concern was for our bread business, but Jesus pointed out,

"This is exactly the point. Concentrate on the gifts I have given you, and give them back to Me to be used for bringing souls to eternal life." I had just read the Gospel and my phone beeped with a text message. I looked over and it was 12:17 a.m. and, for me, the message read "the twenty-third day of the consecration." Yes, I was in the twenty-third day of the thirty-three day consecration to Our Lady. I rarely ever have my phone with me in Adoration, but I thought I should read the text. It turned out to be from *Mary TV* and it started with, *"By God's will, I am here with you in this place. The way to Him may be difficult and painful but do not be afraid. I am with you. My hands will lead you to the very end, to eternal joy."* It closed with a note that read, "Our Lady of Medjugorje, message May 2, 2008. There is no question with instances like this, that God speaks to us, and where He is, His Mother is present when we spend time with Him in Adoration."

There was also a time when my son Jeff and I got into a fierce argument. After an episode like this — but especially with someone I love — I usually go to Adoration.

It was around one a.m. and I was there alone with the Blessed Sacrament. I usually sit on the left side but this night, for some reason, I sat on the right side. The main church entrance was locked tight with two sets of doors that guard you from downtown Boston and the main street. As I knelt in prayer and reflection about my son who lives 40 miles away, I heard a knock on the door. I disregarded it. The knock got louder. My thought was that someone had forgotten their key card to get in, so I got up. I opened the door and standing there in front of me was my son Jeff and his fiancé Mian. I was stunned. Then Jeff said to me, "I saw your car after leaving the concert at Fenway Park, and I wanted to stop and tell you how much I love you and thanks for praying for me."

A lot needed to happen for this to be complete. First, they had to recognize my car. Second, they looked through the main entrance window, and both foyer sets of doors were open for them to see straight in. Then I sat on the right so they could recognize it was me. What really shook me was that God showed us both the power of prayer by convincing them to stop by for this encounter. Here is where the entire chapter concept "Habits That Work For Me" comes together, because after bringing it to my spiritual director, his advice was to "Stop worrying about your son Jeffrey because it's now clear God has this in His hands."

Praying the Rosary and Ignatian spirituality are beneficial in Adoration. The real reason is just to be there spending time with your friend Jesus, and I love to sit there and just be with and look at Jesus. This practice is very Biblical when you look at Holy Thursday and the disciples falling asleep when Our Lord asks them, *"So you could not keep watch with Me for one hour?" (Matthew 26:40)* I feel that by Jesus being there, He is asking me to do the same, just stay and keep watch with Him.

Let me explain Adoration in this way. Most of us own an iPad or iPhone. To make it run at its best performance, we depend on the Apple service team to assist us in getting this product to its maximum potential. The point is, the manufacturer of the device is Apple and they know their product best. Who knows us best? We might think it's ourselves, but I disagree and say it's the manufacturer, Jesus Himself, who knew you before you were in your mother's womb. Eucharistic Adoration is a very important tool in each of our lives, and for me, it's during my time in Adoration that I get the most important answers for the challenges in my life.

The Holy Rosary

Now it's time to reveal the weapon of the Rosary. Some of you — especially the guys — might not think this is a very manly thing to do. "Oh, it's just for those older ladies in church every day." Well, those ladies have a secret relationship with the Blessed Mother; it's one that they share as mothers of us all. The Rosary is where the rubber meets the road. We are talking about the battle against evil here, so if you want to prevail, to protect yourself and your family, you must pray the Rosary, just like your mother and grandmother did. In fact, Saint Padre Pio said, "The rosary is the weapon of these times," and Our Lady says, "*The soul which recommends itself to me by the recitation of the Rosary shall not perish.*"

When my friend Darcie and I talk about the Rosary, she is clear in pointing out that this devotional prayer is the ultimate weapon against all evil. She takes me back to the battle of David and Goliath. According to the story, David, the underdog, had total faith in God when he went to fight against Goliath, the giant. He picked up five stones to conquer the giant. To Darcie, these five stones are similar to the five decades of the Rosary. It's the same type of battle. These five small stones might not seem significant at the time of battle, and the five decades might not seem like much at the time of prayer, but enter Jesus and his Mother and victory is in sight.

Let me now point out historic real instances of the power of the Rosary. During World War II in 1945, the U.S.A. dropped the atomic bomb on Hiroshima, and over 150,000 people were killed. A few blocks away from where the bomb landed was a group of Jesuit priests praying the Rosary. Not only did they survive with just minor injuries, but they had no radioactive sicknesses that affected their health for their entire lives. For over thirty years, more than 200 doctors and scientists examined these men to determine what could have preserved them from this incineration blast. The priests are quoted as saying, "We survived because we prayed the Rosary."

The next example pertains to the Communists taking over a peaceful country in 1947. The Catholic country of Austria went under Communist rule right after World War II. What was this small country of seven million to do against the vast resources of Communism? A Franciscan priest by the name of Father Petrus headed and launched a country-wide Rosary crusade. Between 80,000 and 100,000 people prayed the daily Rosary for peace in Austria. Seven years later on the feast of Our Lady of Fatima, the Communists pulled out of Austria. To this day, not one thing is written in the historic account as to why they left this country of vast resources. The Communists might not know why, but in my mind, it's momentous to understand that Our Lady certainly did know why evil pulled out, and how she was sending us another message on why we should pray the Rosary.

The Blessed Mother herself has promised us all protection and special graces to those who pray the Rosary. She goes further by saying, *"The faithful children of the Rosary shall merit a high degree of glory in Heaven."*

Sometimes Catholics get criticized for praying to Mary. There is a misunderstanding here. The Rosary is a prayer centered on the life of Jesus through his mother Mary. The Blessed Virgin Mary shows us that at each moment of Jesus' life we reflect on in the Rosary, there is triumph because she is the example of total faith and trust in God the Father, her Trinitarian spouse. By praying the Rosary, we are praying with her, not to her.

There are many methods of praying the Holy Rosary.

What is important is that we start praying, now. Let me share with you this special quote from Saint Louis de Montfort, in his book *True Devotion to Mary*: *"Remember to have great love for Jesus, and to Love Him Through Mary."*

For me, the Rosary is a conversation with the Blessed Mother. The first mysteries are the Joyful that completely bring us to Our Lady's Yes: the Annunciation, the Visitation, Jesus' Birth, the Presentation and then the Finding of Jesus in the Temple. The second mysteries are the Luminous Mysteries which were introduced by Pope John Paul II and his love for Our Lady. These decades highlight the Baptism of Jesus, the Miracle of the Wedding Feast at Cana, the Transfiguration and end with the Gift of the Institution of the Holy Eucharist. Then we move to the Sorrowful Mysteries which are the full account of Our Lord's sacrifice: Agony in the Garden, Scourging, Crowning with Thorns, Carrying of the Cross and the Crucifixion. We finish with the Glorious Mysteries which start with the Resurrection of Jesus, His Ascension to Heaven, the Coming of the Holy Spirit, and the last two decades highlight Our Lady's love and dedication to her son: Jesus bringing his Mother to her place in heaven, which is called the Assumption of the Blessed Virgin Mary, and finishes with the Glorious Coronation of the Blessed Mother as Queen of Heaven and Earth. Each mystery has a designated day of the week that correlates to the prayer.

I have read that the most beautiful part of Our Lady coming in her apparitions is her beautiful face. Each time I pray the Rosary, I am touched by the image of Our Lady's face in each mystery. By praying the Rosary, you have been invited to share each decade from the viewpoint of the Blessed Virgin Mary, and how she lived and walked with Jesus each day.

Spiritual Direction

Earlier I mentioned my spiritual director. I believe in the benefits of good spiritual direction because during my competitive golf years, I would not have dreamed of playing serious golf without the assistance of a great golf coach. One of the reasons my game progressed quickly was the no-nonsense approach and advice of my teacher, Shawn Hester.

He was New England P.G.A. Teacher of the Year a few times and I can remember driving hours from Boston to York, Maine just to meet with him and get his advice. He is a special person and a great teacher.

My spiritual director has a bigger responsibility for my soul, and is far more important than my golf pro, but it's a big advantage to have another set of eyes and ears guiding you on your path to holiness.

Father Jeremy Paulin of the Oblates of the Virgin Mary is my spiritual director. He is also the vocational director and does brilliant work at both. The Oblates of the Virgin Mary are like the navy seals of spirituality. It's very important to select a member of an order of priests that specializes in Spiritual Direction. One other great priestly order that does it well is the Miles Christi Community whose name in Latin means 'soldier in Christ.' Both these groups of holy priests are experienced and gifted spiritual warriors.

The spiritual director's role is to be your advisor and assist you in all life's challenges. There are many ways he can do this. In these private, one-on-one meetings, the person will get assistance from the director relating to spiritual questions or just plain life challenges. My spiritual director uses many ways to show me God's plan for me. This is the key. He is not giving me the answer, but he is giving me the tools to find the answer myself. He might suggest some readings from Scripture, a spiritual book or guide, or what I really find works best for me are the examples of the saints. He is there to guide you to the answer through the intercession of the Holy Spirit.

Let me give you an example. Growing up, we were taught and encouraged by most everybody to pre-judge and make fun of everyone but ourselves. This is a bad habit I am still trying to shake. I often pre-judge people I do not even know. So I approached Father Jeremy with this problem and he pointed me to Sister Faustina's Diary Number 163. It reads, *"Help me, O Lord that my eyes may be merciful, so that I may never suspect or judge from appearances, but look for what is beautiful in my neighbors' souls and come to their rescue."* I could never have found this on my own. Reading this the first time is like taking a shot in the gut. It's a perfect fit. I never studied or read about Sister Faustina Kowalska, her diary, or the Divine Mercy apparitions, and now this book is right next to my chair, and I read it and study it daily. I recommend it to anyone who aspires to improve each day. The aid of Father Jeremy allows me to continue to spiritually mature in the ongoing battle of conversion.

One of the best tools I ever learned in spiritual direction is the PRIMA Process of reading Scripture. Here is how Father Jeremy describes it. First (P) stands for that you begin with **Prayer** for your time with the Bible in Scripture, that it will draw you closer to a loving God. Second (R) **Read** attentively, trying to hear the words from God, as if it was your first time. Sometimes it helps to read out loud to penetrate in your heart. Next is (I). This stands for **Imagine** being part of the biblical story you have just read. What would it feel like and how would you react? We now move on to (M). It's important to **Meditate** on what you have just read, what is the message, how does it fit into, or relate to other, biblical teachings? Most important, what do you feel God is trying to tell you in this passage? The Last is (A) which stands for **Apply**. Apply what you have read and learned to your daily life. Follow God's calling and focus on His will for your life with strong encouragement. Take and carry with you God's word into the rest of your day. This whole PRIMA Process works best for me, especially placing myself into the scene with Jesus, the disciples and his loving mother Mary.

One last tip from Father Jeremy from my journal is "Never let a bad experience, no matter how hurtful, move you away from God's unconditional love." This advice from Father Jeremy requires a large dose of forgiveness and love. So bring in a coach, and look to Spiritual Direction if you intend to grow in virtue and follow God's plan for your life.

As we end this chapter, I want to make a point about God putting people in each of our lives for a specific reason. Some of my closest friends sacrificed their time and effort to point out some of these very important tools that worked for them, and helped them to persevere on the pilgrimage of life. I am grateful to Tim Van Damm who pointed me towards Adoration and the Divine Mercy chaplet, which have both been significant in my life. When you read this chapter, please remember this is what works for me. Hopefully you will take a few points and use them in your own life. Maybe you're going to do it differently. One thing is for sure, these practices are for both interior and exterior improvement spiritually. We can never change ourselves, our families, our work, our community, unless we practice these sacraments and prayers. The real key is that we are not afraid to share these practices with others.

Chapter Five Bottom Line

Fifth Gift of the Holy Spirit is Knowledge

In order to live my faith, I had to learn my faith. The six topics in this chapter have assisted me in learning about myself and how can I improve my life in God's eyes, not mine. Each one has a specific role in me growing in virtue and love for God and my neighbor. The funny thing is, I did not choose these specific undertakings. They are a combination of Our Lady's five stones (Mass, Confession, Fasting, Scripture and Prayer) along with suggestions from fellow Catholics who were on a similar journey. Real knowledge comes from the Word of God and He gives us the ability to put His action plan in place. What plan does He have for you and your life? If I can do it, believe me, you can too!

The fifth gift of the Holy Spirit, Knowledge, is often confused with both wisdom and understanding. Like wisdom, knowledge is the perfection of faith, but whereas wisdom gives us the desire to judge all things according to the truths of the Catholic Faith, knowledge is the actual ability to do so. Like counsel, it is aimed at our actions in this life. In a limited way, knowledge allows us to see the circumstances of our life the way that God sees them. Through this gift of the Holy Spirit, we can determine God's purpose for our lives and live them accordingly.

Source:
http://catholicism.about.com/od/beliefsteachings/p/Knowledge.htm

Chapter 6
New Priorities

From my childhood up until my conversion, most of my actions were done in order to impress others or establish success in this world. I had accumulated many connections through business and golf, and my accomplishments made me a deeply prideful person. As you have most likely figured out by now, I am a triple Type A personality, and I was driven to succeed. What success meant to me and my associates was to accumulate material things and status in my social group.

For example, for my entire driving life since 1970, I never owned or used a GPS system for directions in my car. So when we finished the deal with the Montreal bakery in 2002, I felt that it was time to upgrade from my Ford Taurus to an Audi Allroad, fully-equipped with navigational GPS. Each time I needed the navigation system for directions, I would turn it on and hear the voice say, "The navigation is not active." I was continuously getting lost due to this navigation system failure. I pounded my steering wheel in frustration as I pridefully said to myself, "I will do it my way!"

One day, my friend Charlie Fox and I were going to Cape Cod to a new golf course and he said, "Just put the name of the club in the navigation system." I told Charlie, "I don't think they installed it because every time I try to use it, the voice says "Navigation not active.'" Charlie said, "Andy, in order for it to work, you need to put in the address first as your destination." I was really embarrassed and typed in the address and the voice said, "Re-calculating your destination," and off we went with the navigation system working perfectly. The ride was clear, direct, and everything was suddenly transformed for us to get exactly where we wanted on time.

In the GPS of life, God asks me to enter my destination in order for my life's navigational system to work correctly. Before ascending to Heaven, Jesus said that He was going *"to prepare a place"* for us. *(John 14:3)* So our destination is well-known; it's eternal life in Heaven with Him. In order to follow the recalculation of the direction of my life after my conversion, I needed a whole new perspective. The real truth of why new priorities are needed to change my life is that it was precisely my misdirected priorities that kept me away from a direct relationship with Christ in the first place. The navigational system was not active. I needed a full understanding of how to get to my final destination of eternal life with Christ in Heaven. To activate my new system, I had to put my relationship with Jesus Christ in first place, and cooperate with Him in everything. Now I want to incorporate everything, all segments of my life: family, work, community and leisure through and with my new life in Christ. If I am going to depend upon and TRUST in God, I need to put Him first in all things.

In this chapter I am going to share some stories about the challenges and graces I encountered while reordering my life around my renewed relationship with Christ. Warning: it takes enormous risk to rearrange your priorities, and the temptations are often cruel.

Christ in Business

At the time of my conversion, my business had become my number one priority. Running the business was all-consuming and it became my focal point; everything else came second. It was as if my business was running me, instead of me running it. I learned from Scripture that God gives us gifts and talents and what we do with these gifts will mean more in eternity than here on earth. With the new understanding that I am merely a steward of the business, and that it's not mine, that it's a gift from God who can take it away anytime, I began to handle things differently. What I do now is that I still put in 110 percent, but then I let go of the results of my efforts, surrendering them to God. Here is an example.

It was a regular Monday in the bread distribution business. We were meeting with Ryder Truck representatives about the maintenance program, and we were trying to purchase two new trucks for our fleet. We planned on meeting at our facility at 9:30 a.m. This was a big deal with strong implications for both companies. The rental team called and said they were going to be few minutes late. They showed up at 11:05 a.m. and the meeting started much later. This did not sit well with me. We were discussing many points of this program when I looked up at the clock and saw that it was 11:45. I attend daily Mass at noon each day, and this day there were no options to attend another Mass later in the day. I called a time out, stood up in the middle of the meeting, and announced that I was leaving the meeting to attend Holy Mass at noon. I went on further to describe the points I would like the teams to work on while I was away. I said, "I forgive you all for being late and at Mass I will pray for each of you and your families."

Now I was getting some pretty serious looks as I walked out to get into my car and go to Mass. However, as I drove to church, I knew it was very important to let go of the meeting and become calm to prepare for Mass. The kind of action I took is a statement in the business world to members of both teams, and the evil one started to work on me with doubts about leaving them. He pointed out, "You have always attended important meetings. Are you sure they can do it without you?" His main task was to get me to leave my thoughts back at the meeting; this would provide distractions and prevent me from being focused on the gift of the Holy Mass. He hates it when I put God first and practice my faith in front of my business associates. I arrived at Mass and prayed to the Holy Spirit for both teams, and I asked for the Spirit to assist me in shifting my focus to the Sacrifice of the Mass, from what just transpired back at the bakery. Prayer in this situation can act as a light switch: it's dark before you switch over from business mode to prayer mode, but once you do, the graces are extraordinary!

I returned to the bakery around 1:15 and they were all sitting around having coffee with everything accomplished exactly the way God had it planned! Could I have stayed and maybe changed the outcome? Sure, but it's a far better way to trust God and put Him first. I just wanted to hand it off to Him and have Him do with it as He pleased.

I tell you this story first because putting God first is one of the best ways to fight the sin of pride. Pride is defined as, "Excessive belief in one's own abilities which interferes with the individual's recognition of the grace of God." (As I See It, Cody J. Coffey) It has been called the "sin from which all others arise." This definition really defines my life prior to conversion. I was prideful in business, family matters, hobbies and all other areas of my life. I still fight this battle with my pride today, but by putting God first in all matters, the virtue of humility slowly overcomes the sin of pride in my soul.

The next story about putting God first in business relates to the difficulty of being the steward of the people who work for and with you, and the hardest virtue to carry out, forgiveness.

Do you remember Marcus, the young man in Chapter Two, who was freshman in high school and a student in my C.C.D. classes? Well, in the summer of 2012, he had been working with us for almost a decade. During the July 4th holiday, he got into a fight with his supervisor. Now this is really difficult for me because he was like a second son, and he was close with everyone in our family.

The fight was an act of deliberate disrespect towards the whole company and what we stood for. So I called Marcus into my office with his supervisor, to give him a talk and issue him a written warning to sign. I planned to give him just a soft reprimand. However, he refused to sign the warning, and we were both getting irritated and prideful about our opposing positions. I told him if he did not sign this warning, that I would feel he is not looking to improve in this area and that I could terminate him. He responded, "Tough. That's too bad. I am not signing it." I felt awful, but I fired him.

He left my office really mad and he screeched down the driveway in his car. He later told me I should have taken his cell phone away, because it rang in his car minutes later. He was in charge of customer service calls and had all the extension codes at the bakery. That's when the evil one entered our battle, because Marcus took this opportunity to remotely delete $25,000 worth of customer orders. All his fellow workers and my family were in distress. No one could believe this had happened.

A few days went by and, in Adoration, I felt God telling me to forgive Marcus. I resisted God's prompting in my heart, saying, "But what would the whole company say?" God continued to speak to me because everywhere I turned — Mass readings, Catholic Radio — I was prompted with lessons on forgiveness. The following Friday, Marcus' supervisor got sick. Marcus would have been next in line to work, but he was not here. I could not get in touch with my son Jeff, the third in line, so I was the fourth in line to come off the bench and would have to manage the warehouse all alone on a very busy Friday night. I had not done this in years. We had some firm deadlines at ten p.m., just a few hours away; and it became apparent to me that the night was going to be a disaster. I was starting to look like a fool and freak out when I turned around and was shocked to see Marcus standing right in front of me! He said, "I heard that Lou was sick and I found out you were under the gun and very disorganized. Do you need me to help?" I prayed to God for strength and fortitude, and then I remembered my life confession, and how a loving and merciful God forgave me for all my terrible sins. I turned to Marcus and said, "Sure, we need your help, but no guarantees." He said, "I am not here to get my job back. I am here to help you. I want you to know my life would be different without you." With his attitude and experience, the night went smoothly, and all orders got out accurately and on time.

Later, during daily Mass, I turned around for the peace offering and he was there again. I started to think, "What does God want me to do?" It became clear that He wanted me to continue mentoring Marcus by my gift of forgiveness, to help him mend his ways. Does that sound like anybody you know?

After much time of prayer and discernment, I wrote a memo on forgiveness for our company to distribute to all employees, and I hired Marcus back to LaVallee's. The world and our employees probably looked at this as an act of weakness, but I know in my heart that God saw it as a lesson learned. I learned from Him exactly the way to treat another person regardless of what I think the results will be.

A month went by, and Marcus came into my office asking about confession and daily Mass. Over the next few weeks, we attended Mass together and Marcus went to confession for the first time since his confirmation years ago. In order for me to take this action, I had to remember what God did for me by giving me, a sinner, a second chance and His unconditional love in the Sacrament of Confession. Then I had to see Marcus as a person made by God for something special and offer him the same mercy God gave me.

These are stories of how we must look at each situation differently, not as the world sees them, but as God sees them. When we get trapped by the world, we should remember the example of Saint Joseph. God communicated frequently to Joseph in dreams, telling him what to do, and where to take Mary and the Christ Child in order to protect them. Sometimes God asked Joseph to go against the customs of the times, for example, by taking Mary as his wife when she was with child or fleeing Bethlehem for Egypt. But Saint Joseph obeyed God's orders. We must not doubt that God is speaking to us as well. However, to hear His direction, we must remove the clutter. In order to seek genuine improvement in our lives, we must put God's direction first, before all things. Can you imagine what each segment of your life could be like if you began to put God as your first priority in this area?

Here is one last story on business and what I mean about God speaking directly to you to reorder your priorities. In December of 2013, our eight-year tenure with a great operations manager came to an end as he had some personal problems and needed to work closer to home. So as I was attending Mass each day, I would pray to Our Lord to bring us the right people to help our business operate. I started to leave after the final blessing and I heard God say in my heart, "Help that man over there with a job." So I approached this husky man with a cross around his neck, whom I have never seen before, and said, "The Holy Spirit tells me you're looking for a job." He looked at me funny and said, "What did you say?" So I repeated it and he said, "Do not move. I will be right back!" He returned quickly with his pregnant wife who was due in a few months and said, "Tell her just what you just said." So I did, and he hugged her and said, "Honey, I told you God would bring me work if I prayed hard enough!" He came to the bakery the next day and brought his driving record and Department of Transportation (D.O.T.) card. We had an interview and, as it turns out, while growing up in Haiti he worked in the distribution business! We hired him, and I found out from one of the priests at my parish who knew him that he just got married, and he and his wife had been really struggling with no income and a child on the way. This happened only two weeks before Christmas; what a Christmas gift this was for both of us! We both needed to follow the direction of the Holy Spirit. Once I gave God control and stopped looking at worldly results, I found the Holy Spirit influenced everything around me, guiding me in my prayer time, and I started to change.

When I consider my business today, I look at the responsibility of being a good steward of the gifts that God has given me. I am charged with the mission of being a servant leader to all those people who are engaged in each phase of my business. Day by day as I attend Mass and receive the Holy Eucharist, Christ is within me. My interaction with these good people may be the only time that day they have any kind of an encounter with God. So it's up to me to make it right. I must serve employees first, customers second, suppliers and vendors next, with a strong commitment to serve the community as well.

Christ in Women

As I went through my conversion and changed my life, I kept looking for an example of how to put God first. The best example I found was His Mother. Mary taught me that I must allow God to give me gifts I once thought only I could provide for myself. Now I see that it's her Son who provides me with everything I need. Mother Mary directs everything back to her Son. The Mother of God sees us all, and she is persistent about saving every soul. Her love, tenderness and compassion are unforgettable. So it was time for me to look at all women in another way.

You are about to find out firsthand about the kind of man I was, and how deeply ashamed I am about it. Growing up, I am embarrassed to say, I was taught that men were superior to women. I lived this way in my own family and, in my social group, it was a given. In fact, I can remember joining my first country club with a sign over the clock in the men's locker room that said, "A woman can only get so mad." At the time, I thought it was pretty funny, until Our Lady showed me how to think differently about women. I know now that, without my wife Barbara, I would never be the man I am today. Man is a social animal, and I knew I could not exist alone so, in Barbara, I now know that God has given me a spectacular life partner. It is through her that life was given to our family.

It's important to understand that all human creation comes through the women. There are no children without mothers. It is children who bring joy to the family.

I could tell you how I treat my wife Barbara differently now, but I think you would rather hear from her.

"There are several things, big and small, that Andy has done to express his love for me since his conversion. For example, he tells me he loves me every day 'more than anything in the world.'

"On several occasions for no particular reason, he has given me flowers but, most of all, it's the cards with meaningful messages that leave a lasting impression on me.

"The one instance that meant so much was when we went to Italy on a marriage retreat this past May. I am second generation Italian and it was important for me to try to go to the village where my family is from, so I could get a sense of my family history. We were told that the village is so remote that it would be extremely difficult to find. Through Andy's persistence, we realized we were only a two-hour drive to Avellino and the village of Squillani, where my father's family is from. Andy hired a driver and, with much joy and anticipation, we finally reached our destination and were able to connect with my past.

"I think he was as excited as I was, especially when we saw a church in the town square which had a plaque that read all the names of those families who left the Squillani village, immigrated to the United States and ultimately settled in my hometown of Watertown, Massachusetts.

"Andy reminds me from time to time that he is here to serve me. This was a very touching example of his unending love for me."

I knew this was a lifelong dream for Barbara, and I wanted to do everything I could to make sure it was accomplished. Now, I certainly recognize that women are made differently and wired differently than men, but we can be different, have different roles, and still be equal, as long as we recognize God in all people. When we look at Our Lady, she had a far bigger role than any man in the Bible besides her Son. It is a divine role, one that all humanity should respect. It is through her that Our Savior Jesus Christ was born and came to save us. Most conversions and sanctifications come by way of the intercession of the Blessed Mother. We know that the Blessed Mother is the Queen of Heaven and earth, that she reigns over all the angels and saints. Each one of us can know and love Jesus her Son more through her example. It is because of her that all women should be put on a pedestal and treated with great respect in our world today.

Christ in My Family

Let me first say that it's very dangerous to assume our families are going to be fine without the proper knowledge of Who God the Creator is, and how the Third Person of the Holy Trinity, the Holy Spirit, can assist in their lives and lead them to eternity with Him. Your spouse and all the children in your family need to fully understand that they are the most important thing in your life after your relationship with God. As a parent, or grandparent, this will be your biggest challenge. In our world today, we are way too busy with our careers, hobbies — and, in my case, my many friends — to care about our relationship with this divine God in our family.

There is a great example in the Acts of the Apostles when Saint Paul knows he will never see these brothers and sisters again, so he boldly tells everyone, *"You know how I lived among you the whole time...but now I know that none of you to whom I preached the kingdom during my travels will ever see my face again...for I did not shrink from proclaiming to you the entire plan of God." (Acts 20: 18,25, 20)* The message here is this: if you have the wisdom, the knowledge, the grace and the love of God, share it with others, but especially with your family. Do not wait until it's too late.

I am now committing myself to focus more on my children and grandchildren and not on myself. Grandparents have a world of knowledge and gifts to give their grandchildren, and the greatest is love. A man like me who was sometimes too busy with mixed-up priorities is always given a second chance with grandchildren. Barbara and I now have five loving grandchildren. Our best attempt to change the direction of the world is to raise children who, thanks to our example, are taught the love of God, in a family that will do the same for generations to come. Children need a loving father and mother to show them the beauty of God's love. Here is a reflection from my daughter Nicole on how I have changed since my conversion.

"Growing up in a family business, I've witnessed my father at his best and worst. He worked extremely hard and became successful building his business. It wasn't easy, though. The office was in our home and we saw it all. I remember one instance where he had one of those old computer printers with the paper that had perforated edges and the paper was all twisted and stuck and the printer kept going. He was trying to print the invoices for the bread orders as the drivers waited at our door. Let's just say there was a lot of cursing and throwing.

"Now you would see my dad turn to prayer instead of lashing out his frustrations. With his calm demeanor, he is almost someone I don't recognize today. From swearing to praying, he's turned into a humble, unselfish and the most giving person I know. He always says, "I'm here to serve you." But one thing he always had since day one, and never lost, was his love for his family. I became very close with him and named my son after him. Andrew Joseph, "Drew" is now three years old and it's amazing to see Papa spend time with him today knowing that my brother and I did not get a chance to meet our grandfathers. It's truly a blessing."

My grandchildren know that I have a great love for Jesus and the Blessed Virgin Mary. They observe the crucifixes on the wall, the statues of Our Lady and see me praying the Rosary. I am prepared when they ask me questions about the Faith. One time, I can recall telling my grandson Andrew that we were going to erect a statue of Our Lady in the backyard. He was only three years old so he replied, "Papa, do we have to go to church to get her to come here?" He loves Our Lady and I am sure she will protect him like she did me. One thing I always do is to consecrate my children and grandchildren to the Immaculate Heart of Mary and the Sacred Heart of Jesus. This will give them the protection they need to go through life.

In my marriage and family life, in order for me to change, I needed to slow down and gain composure and be a spiritual example by showing humility. This was the biggest challenge for me. Once I realized the evil one wanted to divide us, it was my role to unite us. It's not like fifty years ago when marriage and family were staples in society. Today marriage and family are under attack, so I need to be strong in this protection of my immediate family.

Forgiveness in business is one thing, but to use the same virtue in your family requires an increased level of patience and trust in God's plan. If your family is like mine, they carry grudges for a long time. It's mostly little stuff that turns into big stuff. Love and forgiveness is a must for families to survive.

It's rare that spouses and children are at the same spiritual level. So it's the responsibility of the family member with the greatest influence of the truth of God and His mercy to fulfill the vocation of marriage, and be an example of prayer and forgiveness. I really needed to meet my family members where they were at. As a devout Catholic, I needed to display my interior change, my change of heart and my transformed soul in my actions. This is how we will be judged.

One last thing on family and marriage: it takes sacrifice, time and patience for our families to be faithful in today's world.

After my conversion, my entire mindset was changed by the role model of a woman, the Blessed Mother. In the Blessed Virgin Mary, Jesus was given life and, at death, she held Him as He was taken off the cross. She was tireless in supporting her Son in His mission from His life on earth until today. I knew one thing: the Blessed Virgin Mary led me to her Son and taught me how to be a real man. I now realize my second chance at salvation only happened because of the love of the Blessed Virgin Mary. I treated my life as a commodity, and she valued it infinitely more than I did, and she took an active role in the redemption of my soul. So, because of Mother Mary, I have a whole new respect and dignity of all family members and especially women.

Christ in Entertainment

For years, I spent many hours on the golf course, the racetrack and at my favorite watering hole. I am not saying you should not play golf, but I took it to another level. I played and was a member of some of the best clubs in America, and there was more improvement in my golf game than in my spiritual life. I played over 250 rounds of golf per year, and that's in New England, where there are five months of winter. That means I played golf almost every day. Now that I have the eternal destination in my GPS activated, I can look back and say, "The beauty on the golf course and the friendships are certainly made by God, and very spectacular, but spending time with God, in His real presence is hundreds of times more joyful, peaceful and beautiful." Try it yourself and see.

I used to tape and watch every golf match on TV. Today I rarely watch TV. To me, it seems like a waste of time. A sporting event must be of great importance for me to watch it on TV.

I really do not drink much alcohol anymore, and I spend far more time in Adoration than at the bar. When I walk into the men's grill or one of my old hangouts, I am very uncomfortable about what might happen if I let my guard down. I have learned that it's important for me to avoid the temptation, to avoid the people and places that can easily assist the evil one in destroying my life and, more importantly, my soul.

I have transformed my car radio from sports channels 24/7 to The Catholic Channel on Sirius and EWTN, along with music CDs that are very spiritual and calming. Two of my favorites are "Angels & Saints at Ephesus" by the Benedictine Nuns of Mary, Queen of the Apostles, and "His Love Remains" by Collin Raye. My car is no longer a battleground for the road but a sanctuary. Prior to my conversion, my driving record was Step 31, which means you cannot get a worse insurance rating. My friends would get into my car and immediately open the glove compartment to see my collection of parking and speeding tickets. Most were scared to even get into the car. Four years later, I have a Step 9, which means you're one of the best and safest drivers in the state. This is the biggest area of change in my life, if you ask my golf buddies.

So with the time I used to waste entertaining myself, I now use the gift of time and life to live out Our Lady's messages and to serve God, especially in our ministry, which you will hear more about in the next chapter. If I could make this dramatic change in my life, why can't you?

Christ in Knowledge

I feel the need to evangelize in this book. I want to shout out loud and clear what God has done for me. Before I travelled to Medjugorje, I really did not know my faith. When I returned, I realized that I needed to read and study from some of the best teachers around to gain knowledge and wisdom to communicate the Truth, and live out what God is calling me to do. With the Internet and Catholic radio, we have no excuse not to know our Catholic Faith. We can increase our faith and be properly catechized without spending a dime. So how can we do this?

In terms of books, all you need to do is read anything from Dr. Peter Kreeft or Scott Hahn, two of the great Catholic authors. Both are converts to the Catholic faith and have written many great books on a variety of topics. Read about your favorite saints to inspire you. Some of my favorite saints are my closest friends: Saint Paul, Saint Andrew, Saint Max Kolbe, Saint Louis De Monfort, Saint Teresa of Avila, Saint Mary Magdalene and one you might not have heard of, Blessed Charles de Foucauld. I especially recommend the book, *Fifteen Days of Prayer with Charles de Foucauld.*

I also took classes at Theological Institute for the New Evangelization, or T.I.N.E., in Boston which is associated with Saint John's Seminary. Most people attend T.I.N.E. for the Master's, or Theological, Degree. I attended for the knowledge to gain a deeper understanding of my faith. The classes are informative in every way. I loved the reading assignments, and learned a lot...well, most of the time when Doctor Franks was not piling it on! The times I enjoyed the most were the dialog and questions in class. Being prepared and participating in class was very beneficial for me, and I journaled everything, so I can look back on the notes regularly.

Other great ways of growing deeper in your faith are through retreats and pilgrimages. I try to attend a retreat at least once a year and sometimes twice. The Oblates have a great retreat house just outside Boston in Milton, Massachusetts. I also have attended many Catholic conferences like the Acton University and the Napa Institute. In these events, you are surrounded by many like-minded people who have a vast knowledge of many topics relating to the Faith and are willing to share their experiences.

Christ in Prayer

Just as I have a work schedule, I need to make room for my prayer schedule. What I mean is that there is always time for prayer; it's any conversation between you and God. There are many types of prayer, but the best is the one filled with love. The more love, the better the relationship; the more love, the better the prayer. For me, when I pray, I feel loved, and I want to love as I pray. For the world, it seems foolish to pray at work, in your car, before meals, in the open. I can tell you that prayer begins a new life that goes in opposition to the world, and it's necessary to act contrary to the ways of the world. Teach your family about the benefits of prayer.

Obstacles and Barriers for Godly Priorities

Most of us are wounded and are in pain from past events in our lives. It could be any type of abuse: the death of a loved one, a betrayal of a close friend. You know what I mean. We are not willing to relive the pain and suffering caused by this event. This process hurts, but it's the only way to heal. I learned the best way is to be willing to let the doctor, Our God, in. To release all the pain I carried with me for years about my dad in my life confession was the best feeling! I want to share this with everyone. In one sacrament, the Holy Spirit released all the pain that I carried for years, and opened the flood gates of love and mercy, which led to healing and conversion of my heart. Let us understand that God must open the wound to heal it first, a closed wound is hidden and cannot heal, and it spreads to cause other troubles. If you take anything away from reading this book, I want to emphasize that the process of healing as the love of God renews your soul is very much worth reliving the pain and suffering. Rest assured that you will not miss your sins and bad habits!

When you're trying to live a life of virtue, the temptations are going to be vicious, and you need to put God first to deal with them. This, for me, involved setting entirely new priorities, those recommended by God, which are the best way to live your life.

Today if I have learned one thing, it's to put God first in all segments of my life. How? I am the steward of my life, my family, my work, my leisure, the time God has given me and my community around me. I do this by following the Blessed Mother's lead. Everything she does leads to her Son, so why should it be different for me? In following her, I pray, and the word 'prayer' may be the most frequently used word Our Lady says in all her apparitions. My relationship with Our Lady and her example guides me how to act in all situations. To have true love, understanding, empathy and forgiveness is urgent in our world today. I strive to put God first with the hope that I can convince the next generation to follow her example.

Chapter Six Bottom Line

Sixth Gift of the Holy Spirit is Piety

All the new priorities that work for me in this chapter help me to stay focused on the destination of the pilgrimage of life, eternal life in Heaven.

The sixth gift of the Spirit, Piety, would not have even been possible until I reorganized my priorities and put God first in all things. Before the re-prioritizing, I was lost, and now I have a goal and specific tasks to support me on my journey. These habits of virtue are the new me and how I can show love and forgiveness in each area of my life. Knowing this destination, and the result especially if I stick to God's plan, reminds me of all the reasons I had to reorganize my life. The truth is, it's a constant battle to give up old bad habits and replace them with good ones, and this must be kept up daily. The reorganization was certainly an external act, but the result was an internal improvement in the disposition of my soul. Look for specific things that create similar changes in your life and you will be on your way to re-prioritizing.

Piety, the sixth gift of the Holy Spirit, is the perfection of the virtue of religion. While we tend to think of religion today as the external elements of our faith, it really means the willingness to worship and to serve God. Piety takes that willingness beyond a sense of duty, so that we desire to worship God and to serve Him out of love, the way that we desire to honor our parents and do what they wish.

Source:
http://catholicism.about.com/od/beliefsteachings/p/Piety.htm

Chapter 7
Answering God's Call

It was December of 2010. I called Tim and said, "Between Christmas and New Year's, I want to go back to Medjugorje, to research the fasting bread formula. Will you come with me?"

He said, "If it's anything like the last trip, I wouldn't miss it for the world!" He had been very supportive. All I did was ask him to come and he came! We set up meetings with Fr. Svet and Sr. Emmanuel without any guarantees that we were going to see them. Jim Caviezel sent an email to Fr. Svet saying, "Andy wants to create specific nutritious breads to fast, but he needs to find out what fasting breads are. He also wants to help Mother's Village."

Fr. Svet has been Pastor at Medjugorje since 1997. Following the death of Fr. Slavko Barbaric in November 2000, he became the administrator of the Mother's Village Community in Medjugorje. He also conducts weekly talks with English-speaking pilgrims, usually on the themes of pilgrimage, fasting and the sacraments. He was very close to Father Slavko.

We flew to Medjugorje on our second trip with Tim, my son, Jeff and a few others. On our first morning back in Medjugorje, as we came out of Holy Mass, Maria, who owns the hotel we were staying in and is a personal friend of Father Svet, said to us, "Get in the car. Fr. Svet is waiting for you in Mother's Village." As we drove up towards the entrance, a tall man in a dark brown Franciscan robe was waiting for us. Father Svet introduced himself and immediately asked me if I was a man who takes risks. Everyone laughed, especially my son who said, "Father, risk?? Are you kidding, no one takes more risks than my dad!" After our tour of Mother's Village, we sat down to have lunch with Father Svet and his staff, talking about Fr. Slavko and fasting. I was still trying to figure out what a fasting bread was. Father didn't know what qualified as fasting bread, but he promised he would help me in any way he could with this project. Just as we were leaving after lunch, as I shook Father's hand, he encouraged me to pray to Our Lady and stay close to her Son.

The next day, we went to meet Sister Emmanuel at her convent. Sister Emmanuel Maillard is a member of the French Community of the Beatitudes, and has lived at the Community house in Medjugorje since the late 80's. Ever since that time, she has been spreading the messages of Our Lady. Sister has a great knowledge of fasting; she wrote *Freed and Healed Through Fasting.*

My sole purpose to meet with Sister Emmanuel was to get a better understanding of what was required for a good fasting bread. So I said, "Sister, I'm trying to answer this question: What is a fasting bread?" She said, in her French accent, "Andrew, fasting bread is untreated, unbleached flour with no preservatives, no additives, no conditioners, nothing at all, but it must be good wheat."

If you were standing next to me when I walked into the Four Seasons Hotel in Boston to speak to their pastry chef to tell them about our artisan bread, I would say, "It's untreated, unbleached flour with no preservatives, no additives, no conditioners." It was my elevator speech to a tee! I was thinking, "She just hit it out of the ballpark!"

I was getting ready to leave, and she said, "Andrew, pick a saint," and there was this coffee table in front of her wood burning stove, with strips of paper turned upside down with saints' names on them. She said to me, "Take a slip of paper and pray to the saint whose name is on it." I picked up a strip of paper which read, 'Saint Elizabeth of Hungary.' I just read about her being known for her charity to the poor; she is often depicted carrying a loaf of bread. I had my hand on the doorknob and I was leaving, but Sister Emmanuel said, "Don't leave yet, come back and take another saint for your project."

"What do you mean 'my project'?" She replied, "For these fasting breads you're going to make." It looked like there were 250 slips of paper on the table, and since I hit the jackpot with the first one, I figured that there was no way it would happen again. So I dug in deep and picked a slip of paper from far underneath the pile and as I looked at it, I started shaking my head, the saint's name was Maximilian Kolbe.

After my first pilgrimage, I started to study the saints with a great devotion to our Blessed Mother. I was very familiar with the book *Kolbe: Saint of the Immaculata*. In fact, during a homily at Saint Mary Major Basilica in 1982, Pope John Paul II said of Saint Max Kolbe, *"His love for Mary Immaculate was indeed the center of his spiritual life, the fruitful inspiring principle of his apostolic activity."*

I was about to enter a whole new arena. Saint Max Kolbe was devoted to the teaching of the Blessed Mother, and if we were to be successful in this fasting ministry, we needed to follow Our Lady's inspiration just as Saint Max Kolbe did. So I went back to my room and studied these two saints, and I said to myself, "You can't make this stuff up." Each and every time we sought guidance, we were getting confirmation to go forward. I am so grateful for Sr. Emmanuel's friendship and support. My time spent with her created my full understanding of what a fasting bread formula was, and how we could create this successful experience of a bread and water fast in a ministry on fasting.

After our meeting with Sr. Emmanuel, I was sitting with Tim and my son Jeff and said, "Did you hear what she said, 'untreated, unbleached flour'? That's exactly what we do. We can do this, I can do this!!" It had now been four months since the idea of fasting bread occurred to me during the Rosary in Medjugorje.

At the end of 2011, I was working in my bakery business and it was getting very busy. I was reading, studying, and contemplating, but I really didn't want to do this project. I thought I was too busy at LaVallee's to start another venture. Then I read the Medjugorje book by Wayne Weible and it quoted Our Lady's message of September 26, 1985, *"Dear children, I thank you all for the prayers, for the sacrifices. I wish to tell you, dear children, to renew the messages I am giving you, especially, LIVE THE FAST, because by fasting, you will achieve and cause me great joy. The whole plan which God is planning here in Medjugorje is being fulfilled."*

I heard this at the end of 2011 and I brought this thought to Adoration, and that is how our ministry's name became 'Live the Fast.'

God was prompting me and saying, *"Show me you are serious here. Give up something that's really close to you, something you really love, to help fund this plan."* And He kept prompting me, at Mass, in Adoration, the idea was like a bumblebee around my head; I just could not escape it. So I responded by selling all of my country club memberships except one, to fund *Live the Fast.* I was just trying to follow what God was asking me to do, making a personal commitment. I said, "I know I can do this. I'm going to show you."

Back to my Boston personality, it was as if I was saying to God, "Are you challenging me? I'm gonna show you, I can do this!" As I sold the country club memberships, people said, "What the heck is going on with him? This guy is nuts!" I told my friend and golf professional, Mike Harmon, from the golf club in South Carolina, a great man of spirituality. I made it clear I was leaving the club to join God's team. He said, "You need to do this. Anything to help fasting in the world is important." I thought he was going to fight me about selling my membership and there he was encouraging me to take the risk and work for God!

So we ran a pilot program. I went to specific suppliers, and made sure that the milled flour was not genetically modified, was of a clean label, with no preservatives, no additives and plenty of grains. I used ancient grains, whole grains. Ancient grains are pre-soaked grains and when you taste the grain, it's not as acidic, yet the protein level is the highest level. Every roll our suppliers produce has from four to nine grams of protein.

What I figured out was this: the majority of the breads out there are filled with junk. Most are made with genetically modified flour, which reduces the protein and nutrition level. Man is taking what God has given him in the gift of wheat and diluting it for profit, and for what? Those who want to fast on bread and water are putting chemicals into their system and the side effects are headaches, accelerated appetite and others which prevent people from fasting.

By this time, I had to assemble a team which included first and foremost a spiritual director for our apostate, Father Michael Nolan, pastor of Saint Mary's in Waltham. Father Michael is a great priest and friend who fasts on a regular basis, who understands fasting, and who was really intrigued by the project when he agreed to do it. Tim Van Damm, is an extraordinary friend who witnessed my whole conversion with amazement, and has been there from the start. Like I said in a previous chapter, he introduced me to Adoration, the Divine Mercy Devotion and accompanied me to Medjugorje on my first two trips. Andreas Widmer, a former Swiss Guard under Saint John Paul II, and author of *The Pope and the C.E.O.* is a strong businessman with experience around the globe. He taught me how to determine if your product or service is really and truly good. He says that *Live the Fast* is the ultimate product and service because it will bring people to Heaven. It's because of those two guys that I am writing this book. They coaxed me into it. Another friend, Justin Bell, who has written for the *National Catholic Register*, agreed to be the first *Live the Fast* director.

Right from the start, we realized the secret to successful fasting breads and we knew we could do this. We thought, "When is the most obvious time to fast? Lent, right? If you are not going to fast for Lent, you never will." It was Lent of 2012. We went to the local Catholic media, The Pilot newspaper 1060 AM, the Catholic radio station for the Archdiocese of Boston. Host Scot Landry is always willing to assist a new initiative, but I am sure he had never heard of special nutritious bread for fasting. Our plan was to give away fasting breads and encourage people to fast for Lent. All that was asked in return was that the participants come back and tell us about their experience. In this pilot program, we had 250 to 300 people fasting on Wednesdays and Fridays on bread and water. We created a little community, and everyone shared about their experiences while fasting on our breads. The testimonials were incredible. Nearly everyone said they came closer to God through fasting. Some were never able to fast before; they told us that they had always wanted to fast, and didn't think they could do it. This really convinced us to take this apostolate seriously.

Father Mark Ballard of Saint Mary's Parish in Melrose, Massachusetts said, "I fasted for the first time yesterday on your breads. It was great! It was the most successful fast that I have had in years. I have been telling other priests and laity about you and fasting. I felt such peace and strength and joy about the future."

Other fasters said that the bread was phenomenal. David Franks, a professor at T.I.N.E., the New Evangelization Center, located beside Saint John's Seminary in Boston, is a convert to Catholicism. During his conversion, he fasted regularly. David said, "The bread tasted like cardboard, I couldn't do it. I don't know why. Now I'm fasting on your bread and it's unbelievable." As the testimonials came in, I was thinking to myself, "This is incredible!"

Lent was over; it was the Easter Season, with fifty days to feast and no fasting. It was the day before Divine Mercy Sunday, and I was walking into the Pauline bookstore in Dedham when a lady asked me, "Are you the fasting guy? You have to get this book." It was *The Spirituality of Fasting* by Monsignor Charles Murphy. Monsignor Murphy spent twenty years in the Vatican with Saint John Paul II. Thirty years ago, on February 22, 1980, Saint John Paul II leaned over and whispered into his ear, "What happened to fasting and abstinence in the Church in the United States?" That prompted Monsignor Murphy to write this book. I read it and realized that fasting should be year round. It's not just for Lent; it's for other penitential seasons like Advent.

The next day was Divine Mercy Sunday and I was at Holy Mass. I had just received the Holy Eucharist and I was praying on my knees in Adoration. I said, "God, I want to pray for all those who have fasted this past Lent. I want to pray for all the testimonials we received in our pilot program. It was just so beautiful. Thank you so much." I was taken aback by the response. I felt like something was happening, that God was choosing me to do something and, at first, I said, "No way." But later I said, "I have to do this." I was one foot in, one foot out, but here is when I went all in. I prayed to Our Lord, "I read Monsignor's book yesterday, and he said fasting should be year round. What do You want me to do with this project? Do you want me to continue this just for Lent? What do You want me to do? You know it's busy at LaVallee's and I have no time for discernment, just give it to me, plain and simple." I prayed to Him so intensely that I was almost disrespectful because of my lack of reverence. I left the chapel and went out to brunch with my wife Barbara.

Later that night, at 9:30, I received a phone call. My wife said, "There's a guy on the phone who wants to talk to you." I said, "Who is it?" She replied, "He wants to know if this is Andy LaVallee who lived on 294 Bunker Hill Street on the third floor." So I answered the phone, and the caller asked, "Is this Andy LaVallee who lived on 294 Bunker Hill Street, Charlestown?" I replied, "It is," but I was saying to myself, "Who the heck is this?" He said, "My name is Bill Toland. Does my name mean anything to you?"

The last time I saw Bill Toland, he walked out of my dad's funeral. He was his best friend. It had been thirty-five years, but I knew his voice right away. I answered, "Yes, Mr. Toland, you were my dad's best friend." He said, "That's damn right I was your dad's best friend!"

And Bill said, "And I don't know what prompts an eighty-six-year-old man to call somebody he hasn't seen in thirty-five years, but I was sitting here, reading The Boston

Pilot, and I'm here to tell you two things: One, if your dad was alive today, he'd love what you are doing for the Church, and two, more important than anything else, you need to continue making fasting breads for the Church. The Church needs fasting."

I never imagined that my father would have been proud of me. He was always pushing me, pushing me. He never seemed happy with what I was doing. I desperately needed my dad's approval, but I wasn't given it. That would have saved me a lot of pain and suffering. Father Larry Richards says, "You've got a father wound? Get over it!" It was time I got over mine.

So there I was on the phone with Bill Toland, my wife was standing next to me and I was saying, "Yes, Mr. Toland, thank you. I totally understand. You know what? We have to get together, and he said, "Yes, we'll get together." So I hung up the phone, went to my knees, and cried and cried. Barbara said, "What's the matter? Did somebody die?" I told her what happened, and she said, "I do not believe it!" So I filled her in on the whole story, then I went into my prayer room and I prayed the Rosary. I sat in my chair for a good couple of hours, just thinking about the phone call.

One of the burdens I was carrying around with me was, "Dad didn't see his grandchildren, he never saw what I accomplished. He didn't see me buy the station wagon for $400, he didn't see me get one customer at a time. If he was around, it could have been a lot different, he would have been here, he would have been part of it." I had been carrying that stuff around with me all these years.

So I got the phone call and I realized that Dad was there all along. But now the question was, "Where should I go from here?" I thought, "How do I respond to that call?" and "What is everybody else going to say about this?" Then I remembered, wait a minute, my wife was right there. She saw it in person. I wondered, "What is the real world going to think about this? What are my friends going to think?" Then I said to myself, "Who cares what they think?!"

Do I want to face Christ at the moment of judgment, and have Him say to me, "Wait a minute, let Me get this right. You received Me in the Holy Eucharist, you asked Me for a message, you then said, 'No discernment time, give it to me directly, and simply,' and then I gave you a message from your father's best friend, so that you could understand it, then he told you exactly what I wanted, and, by the way, I gave you forty years of the bakery business experience. Your accomplishments were a gift from Me. In fact, all your gifts and experiences were meant to bring you to this moment; I needed somebody in 2013 to bring fasting back to the Church. I told my bishops, my cardinals, my priests and not many were interested or listening. Andrew, I needed somebody, so I chose you to do this. Why didn't you do this for Me?" That is what was burning in my heart as I was sitting in that chair that night meditating. I said to myself, "It doesn't matter what people think. I have to do this, no matter what the persecution is, no matter what the trouble is. It's my gift back to Him.

Andreas Widmer explained this situation in his own story. He told me, "When I travel, I bring my son a gift like a box of crayons, and here's what happens. Eli, my son, is eight years old. I bring him a box of crayons from Switzerland or Rome and what does he do? He sits down, he starts drawing, he says, 'Daddy, what do you want me to draw?' I say, 'I don't know, make something with it, use the crayons, do what you want to do with it; it's your crayon box. My gift to you is the crayon box. What you do is up to you." So Eli's there, he's thinking and writing and drawing, and he gives his drawing back as a gift. This is your role, God gave you the gift of the bakery business, and this is your crayon box. What you do with it is going to be significant, not to everybody who lives with you in this worldly life; it's going to be significant in eternal life. What you do with this now is going to be important, so you give it back to Him."

One time at Adoration in the middle of the night, I was doing a discernment exercise and I felt Our Lord saying clearly to me, "*Andrew, there are many people who are made by me in the womb for a specific purpose, but few really love me enough to surrender what they have and fully trust in the road I made for them.*" This is probably the most tangible evidence that we human beings are made in the image and likeness of Jesus Christ: that every human being has been made part of God's plan to strive for sainthood and perfection.

He made one perfect human being, Our Lady herself, and he made every single one of us to be like her. He branded us with the letter "M." Find it in both your right and left palm. We were all branded by Jesus Christ, our Father in Heaven Himself, with the letter M on the palm of our hand. To be like His Mother. Just open your palm and look. Everyone has it. That's what Father Calloway taught me as he blessed my apostolate, *Live the Fast*, at the Catholic Marketing Network Trade Show in 2013.

When Bill Toland called me, it put the emphasis on my dad. My father was front and center in my mind as I was attending daily Mass, praying the Rosary, going to Adoration. I heard Our Lord asking, "Are you going to do this for Me?" I went to daily Mass at Saint Mary's where there is a huge statue of Our Lady, and they were singing "Salve Regina." The pilot program was over, and I felt as though Our Lady was saying, "Come to Medjugorje." I replied, "Okay," went straight to my office and cleared my whole schedule. On Tuesday, I told my team, "I am leaving Thursday for Medjugorje and I am going for four nights, five days, that's it." I didn't know what she wanted, but I was going to go." I flew over with some of the materials from the pilot program. I wanted to give it to Fr. Svet as a gift to tell him that the pilot program had worked. I was there for five straight days; I couldn't get near Fr. Svet; he was very busy with tasks at Mother's Village and as the spiritual director for some of the visionaries. My last day, I was going to attend ten a.m. English Mass, and I had planned for my ride to the airport to pick me up after Mass, and I still didn't even know why I was there. The night before, I felt that God kept me awake, so I was praying. Since I was awake, I went to the Croatian Mass at 7:30, thinking Fr. Svet would be there, but he wasn't.

So I prayed the Rosary. Afterwards, I walked towards the rectory and saw Fr. Kevin, a priest from New York, who runs all the English Masses, and he asked me if I was going back to Boston. After I replied yes, he asked me to bring an envelope to the visionary Ivan who lives nearby and I said I would. I asked Fr. Kevin, "Is Fr. Svet around anywhere?" he said, "Yes, come with me."

The next minute, Fr. Svet walked into the office. He said, "Andy, how are you? What have you been doing?" I gave him the newspaper articles about the pilot program, then I spoke of the importance of books and education on fasting. "I want to buy as many of Fr. Slavko's fasting books as you have in the book store. If you have got 1,000 books, I will buy 1,000 books and FedEx them home. I have been buying books off the Internet to give away with the bread during the pilot program, but I can't afford that. It's crazy. We need wholesale cost on books to educate those who are interested in fasting."

Fr. Svet replied, "Wait a minute." He called a woman into his office. "Lydia, Andy is going over to Mass and when he returns, I want you to give him the disc of all Fr. Slavko's fasting books. I want you to give him a one page working agreement that he has the right to reproduce and distribute as many copies of the books as he wants anywhere in the world as a gift from me. He is going to reproduce these books for the purpose of spreading the message of prayer and fasting." Lydia looked at him and said, "Father, are you sure you want to do this?" He replied, "Yes, just do this for me." Then he said, "Andy, I have some advice. Although it's a great book, you don't want the smaller book entitled *Fasting*; you want the last book Fr. Slavko wrote before he died. It's the best gift he's given to all of us. It was written in the fall of 2000; it's called *Fast with the Heart*. He used it for some of his fasting retreats. It has great meditations on the Rosary, Scripture, the Stations of the Cross, fasting with the saints; it's got everything you want in a fasting book. It's the best fasting companion you could ever have. This is the book you want."

In fact, Fr. Svet made a point as I was leaving. He held my arm tight with his right hand, hugged me and said, "Andrew, if you do not do this, no one will. God is calling you to do this for His Mother." I left there thinking that he had made it clear, that I could not let Fr. Svet or Our Lady down.

Now I know why Our Lady wanted me to make this trip. Father Slavko wrote ten books, all with the word 'heart' in the title. He would always use the expression, "Life with Bread" when he spoke about the practice of fasting. For him, fasting had a strong association with the Holy Eucharist.

In April, I took a little sabbatical from *Live the Fast* and in fall of 2012, I said to myself, "I have to do this now, and full-time. Let's get started." I created an office space in my facility at the bakery, and we called it *Live the Fast,* which was to be launched on September 26, 2012, seventeen years to the day that Our Lady gave this message,

"Dear children, I thank you all for the prayers, for the sacrifices. I wish to tell you, dear children, to renew the messages I am giving you, especially, LIVE THE FAST, because by fasting, you will achieve and cause me great joy. The whole plan which God is planning here in Medjugorje is being fulfilled. Thank you for having responded to my call."

The *Live the Fast* mission was going to be threefold: bring back awareness to the practice of fasting, create nutritional breads to fast, and build a community to support each other through prayer and fasting.

I believe Our Lady felt that the launch had to start with Jesus, her Son. When we met with Fr. Michael Nolan, the spiritual director of *Live the Fast*, he said, "Yes, here's what we are going to do. Friday's a fast day; we are going to have Mass, then Adoration from noon to six p.m. Then we can add Adoration on Wednesday from noon to six, and on Friday for the purposes of promoting and praying for the practice of fasting. So Wednesdays and Fridays, we had fasting and Adoration combined.

We launched *Live the Fast* and things went well, so I said to Fr. Michael, "What else do we need to accomplish God's plan?" He replied, "You need a prayer community that is going to pray and fast for you. "

He went on to say, "This is going to be a whole different ball game. It's not like selling bread to the hotels and restaurants. You're going to be attacked." At the time I didn't realize what he meant, but I can tell you I now fully understand what he meant by "attacks." As soon as I entered the arena of spirituality, things started to happen that never happened before in my life. It was easy for me during fasting days to figure out where they were coming from. The evil one never paid any attention to the old Andy, he was real happy the way things were going, but not now. He was going to give me special attention, and that meant I needed to be ready for his attacks. So I said, "Okay. Who do you recommend as a prayer community?" He answered, "Have patience. God has a plan."

A few days after this discussion, late at night, I had a dream. In the dream, I was trying to get into a white tent, and inside the tent was a nun named Mother Olga Yaqob. I had never met Mother Olga but I knew about her work. She came to the United States from Iraq right after the September 11th attacks. A few months later in early 2002, the sexual abuse scandal in the Archdiocese of Boston exploded. She went from one storm in her homeland, Iraq, to another here is Boston. Through much prayer and strength, she was received into the Catholic Church on September 8, 2005. Then in April of 2011, Cardinal Sean O'Malley entrusted to her the mission of establishing a new religious community of sisters in the Archdiocese of Boston, the Daughters of Mary of Nazareth. She has extensive knowledge of, and has practiced the discipline of, fasting her entire life.

Mother Olga is a very compelling speaker and is always in demand. I was blessed to hear her speak twice.

Back to the dream: In the dream, it was clear that I was going to get into this tent. I got in, and just the two of us were seated at a beautiful oak table. In between us was the Monstrance with the Holy Eucharist. Then I woke up. After the dream, I realized that we had to see Mother Olga. She was difficult to get to; she had just started a new religious order and she was very active. Justin Bell set up an

151

appointment for us to meet, and we drove to her convent about ten miles away with copies of Fr. Slavko's book, the breads and my story. When we walked in, she gave us a very friendly greeting.

As we moved into the parlor, I did not know what to expect. I noticed that the next room was the chapel with Our Lord present. Mother Olga said, "Give me your hand." So I put my hand in hers, she wrapped it in the Rosary and we prayed. When we finished praying, she said, "Andrew, I am going to tell you something which is very important." I was thinking, "What is she going to tell me about fasting that I don't already know?" Mother Olga continued, "The Blessed Virgin Mary herself has been preparing me for this meeting with you." I asked, "What did you say? Can you repeat that?" She re-emphasized it. "The Blessed Virgin Mary has been preparing me for this meeting with you. I want you to know that this is her plan, not yours; you're just the tool. She wants me to be close to you in prayer." And we cried and we prayed, and we cried and we prayed. I was blown away.

A month later she came to our first fasting retreat, and I introduced her by telling everyone about our divine meeting from the podium. Mother Olga came to the microphone, gave me a hug and said, "It's true. I had never met Andy before and Our Lady was preparing me for this meeting with him." In Mother's company you can feel the overwhelming love she has for the time with you, and especially for her devotion to Our Lady, the Mother of God. Today Mother and I are the best of friends and her community is growing rapidly. I am most grateful for the advice and direction she provides to me personally and to *Live the Fast*.

We are hopeful for growth in the *Live The Fast* apostolate. We have just been approved by the I.R.S. as a

5013c, and all profits from this book will go to promote fasting. *Live the Fast* has advanced so much over the last year because of the great work of Darcie Nielsen.

Darcie has brought much promise and hope for *Live the Fast*, and I feel rooted in prayer and united by the Blessed Mother. In fact, I see the joy of Our Lady in Darcie each day. I was this businessman who was saying, "How many Facebook hits have we had? How many videos do we have? How many kits are going out? And she said, "Wait a minute, let's just create a prayer schedule." Darcie would be the first to tell you that the more we pray, the more things get done. From the biggest project, to just a caring smile, she puts the stamp of the Blessed Mother on everything she does.

Darcie talks this way about fasting: "Since I came back from Medjugorje the first time, I tried to fast and it was tough on typical bread, and I was constantly going to confession for over-indulging and eating too much bread. I was getting it from stores and eating half a loaf in a day! I said, "This is terrible! So now that I have good fasting bread, I say, "So it *is* possible and more people need to know about this."

Fasting relates strongly to Pope Francis' recent book, *The Joy of the Gospel*. The Holy Father chose the danger of consumerism for his first topic in the apostolic exhortation. He says, "The great danger in today's world, it is permeated by consumerism." In his second topic, he talks about how consumerism, if we're not careful, can affect us in a very harmful way. He explains this by saying, "Whenever our interior life becomes caught up in its own interests and concerns...there is no longer room for others, no place for the poor, God's voice is no longer heard." This is where fasting comes in, we can all fight back by practicing fasting, and I sincerely believe that in order to bring back the joy of the Gospel, and to effectively execute the New Evangelization, fasting is absolutely necessary.

As I said previously, this is why Saint Pope John Paul II said, "Jesus Himself has shown us by his own example that prayer and fasting are the first and most effective weapons against the forces of evil."

I strongly encourage you to take his advice and join the fasting movement at livethefast.org.

Our Lady's messages also call us all to support and pray for our priests, the shepherds. So at *Live the Fast*, we distribute books and breads free to any priest in the country.

Sadly, most people go through their entire lives without knowing their life's purpose or why God has given them the gifts He has. Up until June of 2010, I was a financially secure, self-employed businessman, married for thirty-five years with two adult children as partners in my bread enterprise. My priorities were golf, business, family and God, in that order. Our Lady has a way of showing us a different path, and she certainly did with me. I am forever grateful for her love, and for the direction she used to bring me back to her Son. When I reflect upon this whole situation, it always brings me back to my relationship with my dad. The life confession was a crucial time for healing our relationship.

In fact, on my last trip to Medjugorje, Ivan the visionary asked me to sit next to him during the apparition in his chapel. I felt that this is a seat designated for the holy priest, not me, but he insisted. So, during the apparition, I was crying because for a brief moment, I had seen a trim young man of about thirty years old dressed in a sharp suit. It was Dad. I believe this might be a vision to show me that our relationship has been healed. I often reflect on the phone call from Dad's friend, Bill Toland. I ask myself, "Was this phone call from my earthly father who I had been praying for, or from my Heavenly Father, who just wanted me to realize that, as we go through tough times here on earth, Heaven is not that far away?"

Chapter Seven Bottom Line

Seventh Gift of the Holy Spirit is Fear of the Lord

Let me tie it all in for you here. Fear of the Lord is the ability to serve Him in the hope of doing His will, and find your way to Heaven as you assist others to get there with you. I know in the deepest part of my heart that this is what He is asking from me. He has proven it to me in Bill Toland, Mother Olga and constant communication in Adoration. It only took a simple 'Yes.' It's a big responsibility but, with the tools He has given us, it can be done. "Do not be afraid."

For years I felt I was responsible for all my success. I was soon to learn from this experience that every gift and every challenge God gave to me was to prepare me for His loving plan for me. All my experiences were to prepare me for this time, this moment, to say 'Yes' to Him. It was not what I wanted for myself but what He wanted for me.

What is He asking of you? How has He prepared you? How do you know it's Him asking this of you? How do you deal with this responsibility? How? It all comes down to be open to the prompting of the Holy Spirit.

The seventh and final gift of the Holy Spirit is the Fear of the Lord, and perhaps no other gift of the Holy Spirit is so misunderstood. We think of fear and hope as opposites, but the fear of the Lord confirms the theological virtue of hope. This gift of the Holy Spirit gives us the desire not to offend God, as well as the certainty that God will supply us the grace that we need in order to keep from offending Him. Our desire not to offend God is more than simply a sense of duty; like piety, the fear of the Lord arises out of love.

Source:
http://catholicism.about.com/od/beliefsteachings/p/Fear_of_the_Lord.htm
All Seven Gifts of the Holy Spirit texts are from Scott P. Richert at about.com

EPILOGUE

8-2-2014

Dear Dad,

It's been a long time since that hot day in August of 1975 when you left us. I was so confused and lost; it was very difficult without you being there for me. I was left to find my own way.

You have had a front row seat to see all the good and bad in my life. Little did I know that while I was bitter and suffering, that my Eternal Mother was there protecting me from each foolish mistake I made. I love her so much for being persistent in her concern for my soul.

As you know, there were times I was determined to prove you wrong, when you told me that I would never make something of myself. I remember how mad you were at me. Little did I know your strategy had worked!

Much has happened in 39 years since you passed, and as I look back, your fingerprints are all over my 59 years of life. I want you to know how much I love you, and that I'm grateful for the lessons you gave me and my two brothers while growing up. Real life lessons, that you learned while fighting for our freedom in Korea, or struggling to support a family on $110 a week.

You disciplined me firmly, but impressed upon me the importance of my Catholic faith when I was just a small boy. I remember being four years old on a Sunday morning, in that big green Buick with a bench-style front seat, driving up Monument Avenue. You had your left hand on the steering wheel, and your right arm firmly wrapped around me so I wouldn't fall while we were driving to Saint Mary's for Sunday Mass.

There are so many lessons that this pilgrimage of life has shown me. I guess most people ask themselves, "Why does all this matter?" I realize that few of us, including me, ever gave God the opportunity to work in our lives. When I look back at these events, I know God has blessed me with a loving and loyal family, and a devoted wife whom I desperately needed. All of His gifts were to bring me to my senses and prompt me to be a better husband and father.

So I guess the first lesson I learned is that God is always reaching for our hand to help us, to give us many gifts, but we are looking to Him as well. I just needed to trim away all that was pointless so I could hear His voice and feel His presence.

Just as I was motivated to develop my skills in areas like golf, I learned that a spiritual conversion is very similar. It is an ongoing process, and we never stop improving, but it all starts with the sacrament of confession.

All of these blessings I mentioned, Dad, are really gifts from God, that in early years I mostly used for my own advancement. You know, once I comprehended that God required me to be a good steward of each gift, and I didn't own it, that God was loaning it to me, then and only then could I use these gifts to glorify Him.

It's really funny, and you must be having a real laugh watching as I said "Yes" to God. I went way beyond my boundaries, and have no talent whatsoever to accomplish what He wanted me to do. Most of the time, I am way over my head but He taught me to trust in Him, and when I said, "Yes," my weaknesses are never exposed; just His strength and glory. I hope and pray more people see this and use their gifts to say "Yes" to our Father in Heaven.

One of the other great important lessons you taught me was that all relationships are important. I remember how many friends you had, the lines waiting to see your casket were down the block. Looking back, I now know that God will put people in each one of our lives for a purpose, and we should never underestimate why or how, when it comes to His plan. The best part of this lesson is that God will choose some of the most unlikely people He created to reveal His plan for our life, and for those brothers and sisters in the world He created.

I was such a prideful, strong-headed young man, but once I frequented the sacraments of Holy Eucharist and confession, and prayed the Rosary consistently, things started to change. The real insight came when fasting helped me to identify the purpose of events that I went through in my life. This discipline provided the much-needed spiritual clarity, and purified all my intentions.

I know that in my heart, each of these events were significant to bring me to this moment. Suffering and joy are all part of what we have to go through, but I really had to consider the sequence of these events to see the real meaning, and when I prayed to Him for the wisdom, and knowledge, that is when it all came together and began to live a fulfilled life the way Our Lord wants, not as the old Andy wanted.

Hey Dad, come on, can you tell me who encouraged Jim Caviezel to be persistent in his invitation for me to travel to Medjugorje? Who put Bill Toland up to call me late at night with that important message?

Dad, you're one of the few people in my life as time has passed that might remember that I flunked Junior Year English in high school, and now I am writing a book! As people read the stories in this book, some might say it was all a coincidence. But you know better, don't you, Dad? You always taught each of my brothers that we play a role in each other's life, so I guess it's the same for every family, every friendship, and every fellow worker. The one thing I will never forget was when you said to me one night as I was a complaining teenager, "Andrew, if you're not willing to do something about it, then who will?"

So, I've been thinking about this life journey, and this whole book thing, and it has me trusting in God more and more, and pushing me beyond myself to Him.

I am starting to wonder what life holds for my children and grandchildren. So that leaves one last and very important lesson, Dad. Being a father and raising a family is a big responsibility. An even greater responsibility is being a member of God's Family. He is depending upon each of us to play some big role in eternal life, and it starts here on earth. Up until now I never knew the importance of that role.

So whenever I look to the stars, I feel the deep love of God in my heart and soul, and wonder, if I could only be a husband, a father who gives a good example, and transfers a strong faith and a truly inspiring love for God to our children, so that they will pass it on to their children, then I will be truly blessed.

Those are tears of love you see and, what could be better, blessed by my earthly Dad's prayers and my Heavenly Father's graces?

Praised be Jesus and Mary!
Until we unite in Eternity!
Your Loving son,
Andrew

Acknowledgements

For forty-three years of dating and marriage, my wife Barbara has never said no to one idea or project I proposed. Another woman would have refused most of my proposals, but not Barbara. I know that reliving each of these stories was difficult for her, and I want the world to know I love her with all my heart and soul. Her advice and support made this book possible. I think we are both glad it's over.

As I say in the book, children are a gift. I would never have dreamed that our son Jeffrey and daughter Nicole would be partners in our business some day. I love you both dearly, and pray for you and your families each day. Just ask and I will do anything to help you both.

To my daughter-in-law Mian LaVallee, son-in-law Joe Callaghan, and five perfect grandchildren, Andrew, Lauren, Sophia, Stella, and Lucca, you complete our family.

To my two brothers Bobby and Arty, I hope you guys forgive me for being a know-it-all.

When I first started to tell everyone what had changed in my life and how it all came about, people were mystified. After the continued pressure from great friends Andreas Widmer and Tim Van Damm, it's safe to say the story would never have been told and this book would never have got written, without them. Andreas gave countless hours of personal commitment to assist me in this first-time journey. His friendship and leadership mean the world to me. He is always there for me when needed. Then there was Tim who answered hundreds of questions on spirituality and Medjugorje, provided a divine approach, and I felt like I had the Holy Spirit right there as a brother guiding me in the flesh.

The last enticement to engage in this project to write a book was from friend Teresa Tomeo. After a superb pasta and wine dinner at the 2013 Catholic Marketing Network show in New Jersey, she introduced me to Catholic Writer Patti Armstrong who decided it was best for Leticia Velasquez and I to team up to write this book. Leticia wrote a beautiful book, "A Special Mother is Born," about a parent's call to vocation dealing with special needs children, and her loving experiences with a beautiful daughter Christina. Having Leticia at my side gave me the confidence and courage to share with you from deep within my soul. She did a spectacular job having the reader hear my Boston accent and voice.

Right from the start I knew that if I was going to do this there could only be one person to write the foreword. To me it was going to be all about loyalty and what I learned on the streets of Charlestown. First I wrote the book then I prayed that Jack O'Callahan would accept the invitation. His lifelong friendship and approval of this book means that if O.C. says its okay, then everything is fine. I will let you in on a little secret, he wrote the foreword before he read the book. He is a great writer and I hope he shares his life with us someday.

A deep and sincere thanks to the leader of the Catholic Church in Boston, Cardinal Sean O'Malley, for his trustworthy endorsement.

To speak in terms of Theology, you need a great priest friend to agree to be the Spiritual advisor for this book, and I am forever grateful to Father Sean Morris for your friendship and support. Thanks, Father Sean!!

Sometimes you meet people and you feel like you have known them your entire life, which describes my relationship with editor and book consultant, Ellen Gable Hrkach. She really gets it and is doing Our Lady's work with this manuscript and the direction we are taking this book. Thank you for dropping all your work to take on this project.

Special thanks to Venanzio at Talin.net who designed the book cover and captured the whole story in one design.

A profound thanks to Darcie Nielsen, director at *Live the Fast,* for without her support and guidance many of the ideas in this book might not have surfaced.

A long list of friends gave their advice and criticism. Just like longtime friend Charlie Fox says, "If this story did not happen on the way over here, we have heard it already." Believe me, they are all sick and tired of hearing it. So here goes, a prayerful thanks to each one of you and your peak contributions to the book: Father Joe White, Justin Bell, Charlie Fox, Charlie Howard, Jack McNeil, Victor Rossi, Brad Bishop, Father Jeremy Paulin, Joe and Cheryl Falco, Father Bill Brown, Tony Lyons, Jack Pasienza, Pete Whinfrey, Mike Harmon, Father Michael Nolan, Father Dermot Roache, Father Tom Hart, Magnus McFarlane, Jim and Kerri Caviezel, Mike Sweeny, Randy Hain, Jack Proctor, Christian Nielsen, Ed Casey, Jim Goodfella, Allen Hunt, Dean and Carole Burpee, Bobby Talbot, Maria Cusack, Diane Krolo, Kevin McCarthy, Mike Sullivan, James Davis, Artie Boyle, Kevin Gill, Rob Griffin, Arthur S. Demoulas, Meghan Martin, Mother Olga, Ambassador Raymond Flynn, Drew Mariani, Father Tim Gallagher, Bucky MacKinnon, Marcia Walsh, Mary Bernadette, Bob Frazier, Shawn Hester, Bob Allard, Joe Gemmell, Anthony Nadar, Paul Toland, Maria Paulic, Father Jozo Grbes, Father Svetozar Kraljevik and Christine Watkins. Special thanks to Scot Landry and Elizabeth Alton, whose recommendations were remarkable.

Most of all, I am grateful to you, the reader, who took the time to read this memoir.

Turning to His disciples, He spoke to them by themselves, "Blessed are the eyes that see what you see, for I tell you that many prophets and kings wanted to see what you see, and never saw it; to hear what you hear, and never heard it." (Luke 10:23-24)

Look, I am just a bread man, a nobody, but I know in my Heart that God has spoken to me, and is looking to speak to you. Strip away the things of the world and allow Him to transform your life!

I pray that some of these stories and examples will inspire you to listen to the movement of the Holy Spirit in each of your own lives. Rest assured that you are all in my prayers. Praised be Jesus and Mary!!!

Andrew LaVallee

February 11, 2015,
Feast of Our Lady of Lourdes

RECOMMENDED READING

True Devotion to Mary (With Preparation for Total Consecration) by St. Louis de Montfort, translated by Reverend Frederick Faber, Robson, Levey, and Franklyn, London, UK, 1863

The New American Bible, Saint Joseph Edition (Approved by U.S. Council of Bishops), Catholic Book Publishing, June 1990

Aim Higher: Spiritual and Marian Reflections of St. Maximilian Kolbe by Maximilian Kolbe, Franciscan Marytown Press, 1994

Kolbe, Saint of the Immaculata by Francis M. Kalvelage, Ignatius Press, June 2002

Be a Man by Fr. Larry Richards, Ignatius Press, 2009

Fast with the Heart by Fr. Slavko Barbaric, The Medjugorje Web, 2012

In the School of Love by Fr. Slavko Barbaric, Faith Pub Company, 1997

Give Me Your Wounded Heart: Confession Why and How, Father Slavko, Medjugorje Web, 2012

Medjugorje: The Last Apparition-How it Will Change the World by Wayne Weible, New Hope Press, First Edition, 2013

Lord Have Mercy: The Healing Power of Confession by Scott Hahn, Image Publishers, First Edition, 2005

How to Win the Culture War: A Christian Battle Plan for a Society in Crisis by Peter Kreeft, IVP Books, 2009

Yes or No: Straight Answers to Touch Questions About Christianity by Peter Kreeft, Ignatius Press, 1991

Rediscover Catholicism: A Spiritual Guide to Living with Passion and Purpose by Matthew Kelly, Beacon Publishing, Second Edition, 2011

The Cost of Discipleship by Dietrich Bonhoeffer, Touchstone, First Edition, 1995

The Pope and CEO: John Paul II's Leadership Lessons to a Young Swiss Guard by Andreas Widmer, Emmaus Road Publishing, 2011

An Ignatian Introduction to Prayer by Timothy M. Gallagher, OMV, Crossroad Publishing Company, 2008

Great Lent: Journey to Pascha by Alexander Schmemann, St Vladimirs Seminary Press; 2nd edition, 1974

The Purpose Driven Life by Rick Warren, Zondervan, 2002

Noise: How Our Media-Saturated Culture Dominates Live and Dismantles Families by Teresa Tomeo, Ascension Press, 2012

Journey to Heaven: A Road Map for Catholic Men by Randy Hain, Emmaus Road Publishing, 2014

The Coming Revival: America's Call to Fast, Pray and "Seek God's Face" by Bill Bright, New Life Publishing, First Edition, 1995

Saint John Paul The Great: His Five Loves by Jason Evert, Totus Tuus Press, 2014

Charity in Truth: Caritas in Veritate by Pope Benedict, Ignatius Press, 2009

The Spirituality of Fasting: Rediscovering a Christian Practice by Charles M. Murphy, Ave Maria Press, 2012

Six Months to Live: Three Guys on an Ultimate Request for a Miracle by Arthur Boyle and Eileen Boylen, Crossroad Publishing Company, 2014

15 Days of Prayer with Charles DeFoucauld by Michael Lafon, New City Press, 2008

As I See It: A Compelling Insight Into the Existence of God, by Cody Coffey, Create Space Independent Publishing, 2013

Catholics Come Home: God's Extraordinary Plan for Your Life by Tom Peterson, Image Publishing, 2013

To Love Fasting: the Monastic Experience by Adalbert De Vogue (author), John B. Houde (Translator), Saint Bede's Publishing, 1993

Full of Grace: Miraculous Stories of Healing and Conversion through Mary's Intercession by Christine Watkins, Ave Maria Press, 2010